Family HISTORY
SCRAPBOOKING

by BECKY HIGGINS

BECKY DID IT AGAIN!
by Lisa Bearnson

My 12-year-old son, Collin, recently had to write an essay on a relative who immigrated to the United States. After doing a little research, both Collin and I were so touched and inspired by the stories of his great-great-great-grandfather J. H. D. Victor Tieman; we knew Collin's project would have to focus on him.

Collin's research project was only the beginning of a glimpse into the life of an incredible man. Imagine this: Victor arrived in the United States at the age of 17, with everything he owned tied up in a red handkerchief. He only had 50 cents in his pocket. He worked long hours washing dishes in order to return home to Germany, where he married his childhood sweetheart. Eventually, they returned to the United States together, to homestead in Missouri and raise 12 children.

Victor's stories captured my attention and my heart. I knew I wanted to create a scrapbook page that told Victor's story *and* linked Collin to Victor. (After all, many of the things that Collin now enjoys are directly linked to Victor's hard work, sacrifice and love for his family.)

But I'll admit it—deciding what to do next was the hard part. How should I tell the story? What photographs should I use? Where could I go for missing pieces of information? And how should I present the information on a scrapbook page that did justice to the stories I wanted to tell?

Who came to my rescue? Becky Higgins, of course! I've known Becky for almost a decade, and she's one of the most organized people I know. She's also passionate about family history. She helped answer all of my questions—and in this book, she'll be there to help you, too.

Join with me in getting started now. Let's not allow the "Victor" photos and stories we all have become faded and lost. There's no better time than the present to get started. This book will hand-hold you through the process—guaranteed. Thanks, Becky!

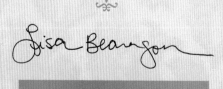

Contents

8

One: **GATHER**

Gather the photographs and documents you need to get started on your project.

36

Two: **SORT**

Sort your family history materials into manageable categories.

60

Three: **PREPARE & ORGANIZE**

Prepare and organize your photographs and documents for scrapbooking.

84

Four: **DISCOVER**

Discover the missing information you need to tell your stories.

110

Five: **PRESENT**

Present and scrapbook your family history in a timeless way.

136

Six: **BONUS**

More answers to your family history questions.

Question:
*Becky, how did you get interested
in family history?*

For as long as I can remember, I've had a strong interest in preserving my memories (well, hello—that explains that whole scrapbooking thing!). As a young girl, I would sit on the floor and tape-record my audio diary. I have a handful of journals. I've always loved taking pictures of the people in my life, my house, the things I love. I even got my friends to go along with my "let's write our life stories on paper" moments. Don't worry—we still talked about boys, played with make-up, listened to music and rode our bikes.

As I got older, I developed more of an interest in pictures, journals and memories from my ancestors. This is largely due to my dad's inherent love for personal and family history. He wrote his autobiography a couple of decades ago. Dad has spent many hours researching and finding ancestors. My parents have traveled to Germany in the quest for returning to his roots. Dad even compiled a family history book to share with our family, including many distant relatives. I'm very fortunate—so much of our family's history has been discovered and collected by my parents and grandparents.

The documents, biographies, photographs and stories from my family have captured my interest. Of course, this interest carries over to my husband's heritage as well. I've enjoyed learning about those who have gone before us. I love learning about their experiences, understanding their values and appreciating their uniqueness.

Question:
*How do I get past feeling absolutely
overwhelmed and get started on my family history?*

I know. It can be daunting. Especially if you have boxes upon boxes of
stuff and mostly unlabeled photos. Just start with one particular family or
individual and zoom in on that person or family. Then move on to others.
Start with basic information and go from there. Once you get started, I
bet you'll be delighted with the process. You'll naturally want to learn
more. You'll catch a bit of the family history scrapbooking bug, and you'll
become passionate about preserving your family memories.

Sunday dinner. Always the same thing in the Johnson home. Esther would prepare hamburger patties (cooked in a pan on the stove, not on an outdoor grill), real mashed potatoes, cream gravy made from scratch, and peas. And there was usually company. They invited others to join them, mostly the local missionaries. Esther made everyone at the dinner table happy. She cooked the "southern" way, with lots of butter and grease from bacon or fatback. She learned the art of cooking from her own mother and grandmother and Anne & Pearlie (her aunts). Even Grandma Knight (her mother-in-law) cooked the "southern" way.

This photo was taken in the dining room of Jake & Esther's home in Takoma Park, MD as Esther was setting the table. The hutch was Grandma Knight's, as well as the wash bowl and pitcher sitting on top. Vicki also remembers the chairs because they swiveled and they used to spin around on those chairs until they were about sick!

esther, the
homemaker

{
Question:

*Becky, how will this book help me
get a handle on my family history?*
}

Thinking about "scrapbooking your family history" can be enough to make you want to throw your hands up. It just feels like too much to swallow. But when you break it down and understand how to do it in stages, it not only becomes more manageable, but also enjoyable. It's my goal to help you feel more organized, more interested and more motivated about your family history. I'm going to share all kinds of great tips with you on the process of gathering, sorting, preparing and organizing, discovering and presenting. We're in this together. You and me. We both want to preserve our heritage in a format that will be fun to create and enjoyable to read.

As with most things in life, there is a time and a season for everything. Maybe now is the time to do your family history. If it is, I sincerely hope this book becomes a valuable resource to help you along the way. Get your family involved, too. It is, after all, about family. Let's get started! To see more pages from my albums, check out www.creatingkeepsakes.com/becky

general information about
ROY

His mother died young, leaving his father to raise three young children. At almost 20 years old he married Henrietta, who was also of solid German stock. When their first child was still an infant, they packed up what they had and took the train to barren northwestern South Dakota, where they homesteaded.

1931

1960

Parents: Adolf August Allgaier & Sarah Hansing Allgaier

Birth: 24 September 1885

Birthplace: Kankakee, Kankakee, Illinois

Married: Henrietta Wilhelmina Tammen (same age and also from Illinois)

Marriage date: 26 August 1905

Marriage place: Kankakee, Kankakee, Illinois

Children:
Earl LeRoy Allgaier (born 8.7.1908)
Evelyn Vivian Allgaier (born 2.13.1914)

Died: 10 March 1978

Place of death: Miller, Hand, South Dakota

---

in her Kitchen

1942

1977

Frozen, chocolate-covered bananas. That's the most vivid memory I have when I think of Grandma Allgaier in her kitchen. She seemed to always make this treat for us kids when we visited her home. Oh, I loved the sight of her pulling them out of her freezer to share with us. And I love these pictures of her in her kitchen, taken about 3 ½ decades apart. First as a young wife & new mother and later as an aging grandmother to many, still "doing her thing" in the same kitchen.

[May 1918]
George (10) &
Leonard (13)
STEWART
brothers

*N*o doubt about it, starting your family history work can be intimidating. Maybe you have a shoebox of old letters in the closet and a drawer full of photographs in your living room—and no idea how to begin. In this chapter, I'll share the first step to making family history work fun and fulfilling: gathering photos, memorabilia, documents, information and more.

Before you begin the gathering process, create a "home base" for your items. Choose a location that will be safe from children, pets, sunlight, humidity and anything else that could harm those irreplaceable objects. Your home base might be a desk in your office, an armoire in your family room or even a spot in your bedroom closet.

Once you've created a central location for your family history information (let's call it your "family history corner"), you'll know exactly where to put things as you acquire them. Collect photographs, documents, letters, biographies, memorabilia, medals and more and store them in this central location.

The good news about your family history corner is that you'll know exactly where to go to find important information. When your kids ask you about life before the Internet, you can turn to your family history corner and pull out your old photographs. Wondering where your great-grandparents' love letters are? The family history corner, of course.

No matter how much or how little you have
at this point, it's worth taking the time to create a
designated home for these valuable items.

This step alone—creating a central location for your items—will bring you peace of mind and a sense of order and accomplishment. And with this task completed, you're ready to delve into the gathering process. Read on to learn how to find information, how to ask questions, how to get your family members involved and more.

{ Question:
*Becky, how do you organize your
family history information?* }

I organize my information both by family and by individual family member. I keep a series of binders and folders where I can easily store information about each person.

I also keep both completed and incomplete pages in my albums. This keeps all of my information about each family and family member in one place. If I get a new photograph of my grandma, I'll slip it in a sheet protector and add it to her album. When I'm ready to scrapbook that photograph, I know exactly where to find it.

Question:

*How do I decide on an organizational system
for my family history project?*

Start by thinking about the scope of your project and what kind
of project you want to create. For example, are you interested in
creating a single mini album, or do you want to create a complete
family history library?

Another important consideration? Take a look at the number of
photographs and documents you have in your possession. Some
of my friends have boxes and boxes of materials, but another
friend has only an envelope with a few photographs tucked
inside. The number of items you have might dictate what type of
organizational system you use.

Whatever system you choose, start with one that's easy to use and
that's easily expandable so you can add new information as you
gather it. A great way to start, no matter how big or small the
scope of your project, is with a system of accordion-style folders—simply designate a section for each family member.

Checklist

Family history work is packed with possibilities! Your project can be anything you'd like—from a scrapbook of family stories to a complete family history library. Before you start working, take a minute and decide what sort of project you want to create. Here are 10 ideas to consider:

1. A complete family history library with a binder for each family in your history

2. A scrapbook filled with a summary of the people in your life

3. An album full of family stories and snapshots

4. A recipe album that features recipes passed down through your family

5. A tribute album that honors a person or couple in your family

6. A mini album that answers most-often-asked family questions

7. A family tree album that focuses on the structure of your family tree

8. A question-and-answer album that answers questions about your family members and their lives

9. A children's storybook with photographs of ancestors and interesting facts about them

10. An "all about me" album that traces your connection (genetics, interests) to past family members

Choosing Supplies

Question:

*On a practical level, what supplies should I purchase
to organize my family history?*

The organizational supplies you purchase will depend on the scope of your project. Consider acid-free file folders for storing photographs and documents, and acid-free boxes for larger items. You'll also need archival-quality supplies to use when you begin to create your family history pages, including archival-quality pens and cardstock. I'll talk about this a bit more in Chapter 5, but for now, no matter what, make sure your materials are high quality and acid free.

Your computer is also an invaluable "supply" for working on family history. It will come in handy for doing Internet research, sharing information with other relatives, printing scans of old photographs, and even typing and printing journaling for your scrapbook pages.

{ *Question:*
How do I go about setting up
interviews with my relatives? How should I
conduct these interviews? }

First, call or e-mail relatives and set up a time to talk with them about family history. When I approached my great-aunt Virgie, I explained that I wanted to ask her a few questions and promised not to keep her more than a few minutes. I made sure to let her know that I cared about her, was interested in preserving her memories and respected her time.

As you conduct your interviews, keep the focus positive and upbeat. Make sure the environment is relaxed, and let your relatives lead the conversations. Yes, you may have a list of 20 questions to ask, but you might be pleasantly surprised at the direction the answer to your first question takes. Show interest, be a good listener, and let your relatives tell you what they want you to hear. If you notice that an older relative is getting tired, keep your promise to keep it brief and ask permission to set a date for another interview.

One more tip—some people feel intimidated by the word "interview." You might ask relatives if they'd like to chat about family history or if they'd be interested in having a conversation about family history. This sort of friendly approach might help relatives relax and enjoy the process a bit more.

Checklist

10 INTERVIEW QUESTIONS

Need a starting place? The 10 questions listed here will help you formulate your own questions to ask your relatives. You'll find more lists of questions throughout this book.

1. What is your full name? Have you ever had a nickname?

2. When and where were you born?

3. Did you live close to other family members?

4. Where did you grow up?

5. What do you remember best from your childhood home?

6. Did you move as a child? If so, where?

7. What is your earliest childhood memory?

8. How many brothers and sisters did you have?

9. What kind of games did you play growing up?

10. What was your favorite toy and why?

Question:
*I've never conducted an interview before.
Can you give me some tips?*

My good friend, Delta Stacey, loves family history. She's interviewed over 30 people and has some great tips for conducting family history interviews. Here are her favorites:

❊ Try to interview people in person whenever you can. This is the best way to ensure you hear the entire story instead of just the parts your family member decided to write down for you. Also, during a face-to-face interview, it's easy to ask follow-up questions and get answers you might have otherwise missed.

❊ As you conduct interviews, ask your relatives if they can think of any other family members who might be willing to share their perspective on the same story.

❊ Take frequent breaks. Interviewing can be tiring for you and your relatives— keep it fun and fresh.

❊ If possible, give relatives a short list of questions ahead of time. This will give them time to process the information and to start reminiscing about their family history.

❊ Ask open-ended questions, such as, "I've heard something about Aunt Mabel's pumpkin pies …" These types of questions usually elicit the best stories!

"What can you tell me about this picture?" I ask my mom.

"What do you want to know?"

"Everything."

What we remember from our childhood we remember forever.
-Cynthia Ozick

She would spend her summer days playing in this bucket filled with water. She was only three, and this activity not only entertained, but kept her away from the busy street and from making a muddy mess.

She would sit and watch her parents work in the yard, or the people in the neighborhood go by and some days she could even get her older brother Richard to play with her.

She would 'accidentally' spray her mom with the water and giggle innocently. And she would remember this as a very happy time of her life.

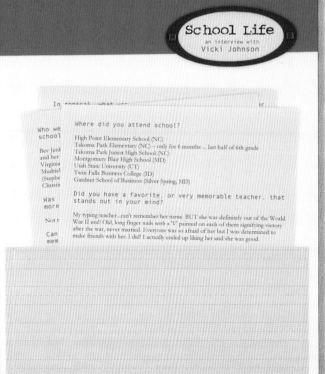

Mom and Uncle Richard, Summer 1958

School Life
an interview with
Vicki Johnson

In general, what was

Where did you attend school?

Who we school

High Point Elementary School (NC)
Takoma Park Elementary (NC) – only for 6 months ... last half of 6th grade
Takoma Park Junior High School (NC)
Montgomery Blair High School (MD)
Utah State University (UT)
Twin Falls Business College (ID)
Gardner School of Business (Silver Spring, MD)

Bev Jenk
and her
Virginia
Mudricl
(Stephe
Christi

Did you have a favorite, or very memorable teacher, that stands out in your mind?

Was
more

My typing teacher...can't remember her name. BUT she was definitely out of the World War II era!! Old, long finger nails with a 'V' painted on each of them signifying victory after the war, never married. Everyone was so afraid of her but I was determined to make friends with her. I did! I actually ended up liking her and she was good.

Not r

Can
mem

{ **Question:**
*How can I use e-mail to gather
family history information?* }

E-mail is a great way to share and trade information with techno-savvy relatives. If you choose to conduct interviews via e-mail, ask open-ended questions to elicit information. And be sure to ask only one or two questions per e-mail; otherwise, the sheer volume of typing can get overwhelming quickly.

Several years ago, I asked my parents to e-mail me, in their own words and writing style, about how they met each other, fell in love and got married. I left it open-ended so they would share whatever details they wanted. The result is a treasured document: their love story.

Also, remember to print out your e-mail responses and add them to your organizational system. You don't want to waste precious time searching for those answers in your e-mail box. If possible, print your answers in archival-quality ink so you can use them directly on a scrapbook page.

Connelly + Russo = German. (huh?)
We were on the playground at school the other day and a friend's mom said "Wow, Aidan must be German. Am I right?" My first thought was "Huh? How the heck does she get German from 'Aidan Russo.'" She went on to say it was because he was so big and...um...big. I explained that I was Irish and Vic was Italian.
But you know what? She was right. I started thinking about it, and here's the family's genetic breakdown.
• My paternal grandmother = Kreplin. German.
• My paternal grandfather = Connelly. Irish.
• My maternal grandmother = Dannenburg. German.
• My maternal grandfather = Frear. Dutch (Which is sort of like German, right?)
• Vic's maternal grandparents = Grimm. 100% German.
• Vic's paternal grandparents = Russo. 100% Italian.
Sooo, doing my (admittedly bad) math, that makes my kids 4/6 (aka 2/3rds - thank you, Vic) German. Wow. And to think I'd been blaming Aidan's size on my Dad for all these years. Guess from now on, I can say "He's just hearty German stock." I'm still claiming to be Irish, though, seeing as it's the only excuse I have for my bad temper, complete lack of patience and love of all things potato.

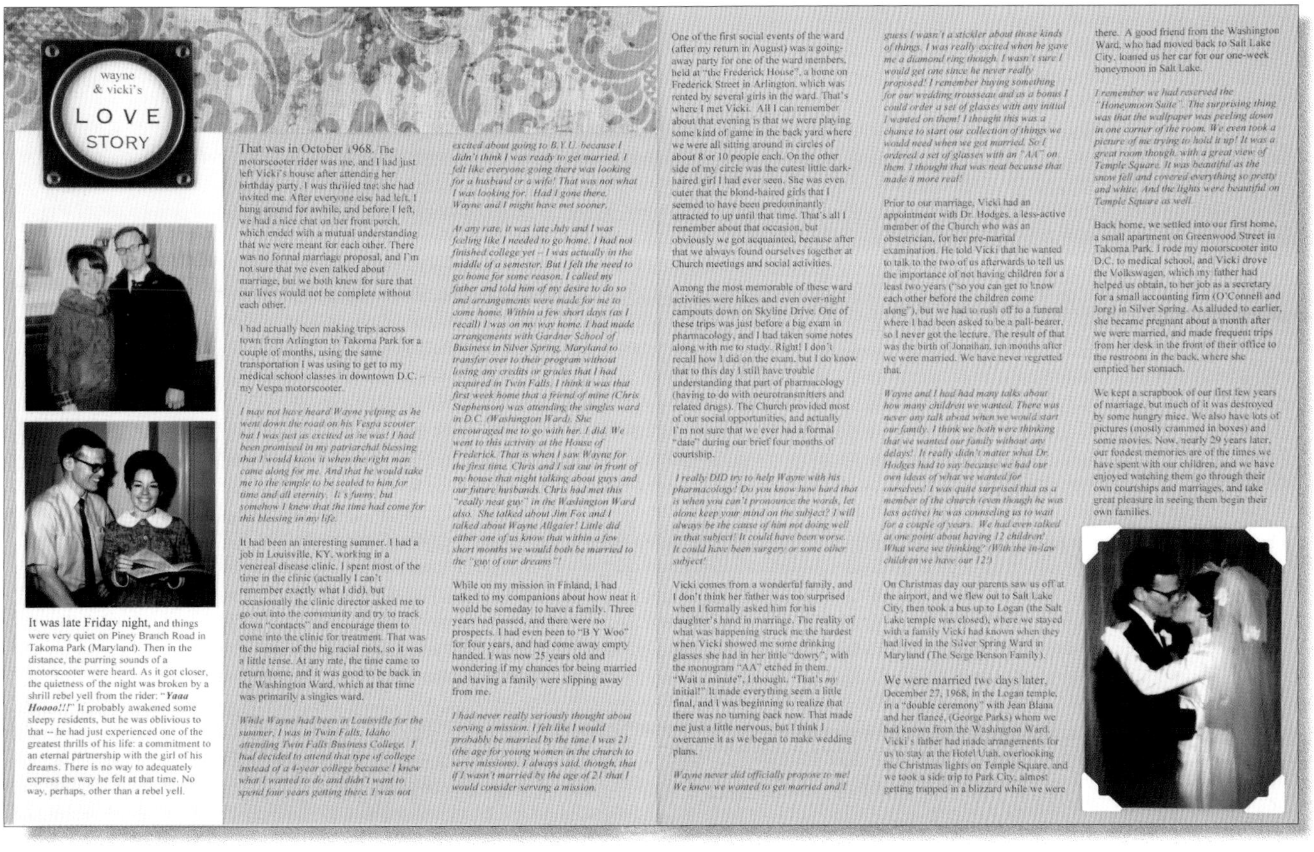
wayne & vicki's LOVE STORY
It was late Friday night, and things were very quiet on Piney Branch Road in Takoma Park (Maryland). Then in the distance, the purring sounds of a motorscooter were heard. As it got closer, the quietness of the night was broken by a shrill rebel yell from the rider: "Yaaa Hoooo!!!" It probably awakened some sleepy residents, but he was oblivious to that -- he had just experienced one of the greatest thrills of his life: a commitment to an eternal partnership with the girl of his dreams. There is no way to adequately express the way he felt at that time. No way, perhaps, other than a rebel yell.
That was in October 1968. The motorscooter rider was me, and I had just left Vicki's house after attending her birthday party. I was thrilled that she had invited me. After everyone else had left, I hung around for awhile, and before I left, we had a nice chat on her front porch, which ended with a mutual understanding that we were meant for each other. There was no formal marriage proposal, and I'm not sure that we even talked about marriage, but we both knew for sure that our lives would not be complete without each other.
I had actually been making trips across town from Arlington to Takoma Park for a couple of months, using the same transportation I was using to get to my medical school classes in downtown D.C. – my Vespa motorscooter.
I may not have heard Wayne yelping as he went down the road on his Vespa scooter but I was just as excited as he was! I had been promised in my patriarchal blessing that I would know it when the right man came along for me. And that he would take me to the temple to be sealed to him for time and all eternity. It's funny, but somehow I knew that the time had come for this blessing in my life.
It had been an interesting summer. I had a job in Louisville, KY, working in a venereal disease clinic. I spent most of the time in the clinic (actually I can't remember exactly what I did), but occasionally the clinic director asked me to go out into the community and try to track down "contacts" and encourage them to come into the clinic for treatment. That was the summer of the big racial riots, so it was a little tense. At any rate, the time came to return home, and it was good to be back in the Washington Ward, which at that time was primarily a singles ward.
While Wayne had been in Louisville for the summer, I was in Twin Falls, Idaho attending Twin Falls Business College. I had decided to attend that type of college instead of a 4-year college because I knew what I wanted to do and didn't want to spend four years getting there. I was not excited about going to B.Y.U. because I didn't think I was ready to get married. I felt like everyone going there was looking for a husband or a wife! That was not what I was looking for. Had I gone there, Wayne and I might have met sooner.
At any rate, it was late July and I was feeling like I needed to go home. I had not finished college yet – I was actually in the middle of a semester. But I felt the need to go home for some reason. I called my father and told him of my desire to do so and arrangements were made for me to come home. Within a few short days (as I recall) I was on my way home. I had made arrangements with Gardner School of Business in Silver Spring, Maryland to transfer over to their program without losing any credits or grades that I had acquired in Twin Falls. I think it was that first week home that a friend of mine (Chris Stephenson) was attending the singles ward in D.C. (Washington Ward). She encouraged me to go with her. I did. We went to this activity at the House of Frederick. That is when I saw Wayne for the first time. Chris and I sat out in front of my house that night talking about guys and our future husbands. Chris had met this "really neat guy" in the Washington Ward also. She talked about Jim Fox and I talked about Wayne Allgaier! Little did either one of us know that within a few short months we would both be married to the "guy of our dreams"!
While on my mission in Finland, I had talked to my companions about how neat it would be someday to have a family. Three years had passed, and there were no prospects. I had even been to "B Y Woo" for four years, and had come away empty handed. I was now 25 years old and wondering if my chances for being married and having a family were slipping away from me.
I had never really seriously thought about serving a mission. I felt like I would probably be married by the time I was 21 (the age for young women in the church to serve missions). I always said, though, that if I wasn't married by the age of 21 that I would consider serving a mission.
One of the first social events of the ward (after my return in August) was a going-away party for one of the ward members, held at "the Frederick House", a home on Frederick Street in Arlington, which was rented by several girls in the ward. That's where I met Vicki. All I can remember about that evening is that we were playing some kind of game in the back yard where we were all sitting around in circles of about 8 or 10 people each. On the other side of my circle was the cutest little dark-haired girl I had ever seen. She was even cuter that the blond-haired girls that I seemed to have been predominantly attracted to up until that time. That's all I remember about that occasion, but obviously we got acquainted, because after that we always found ourselves together at Church meetings and social activities.
Among the most memorable of these ward activities were hikes and even over-night campouts down on Skyline Drive. One of these trips was just before a big exam in pharmacology, and I had taken some notes along with me to study. Right! I don't recall how I did on the exam, but I do know that to this day I still have trouble understanding that part of pharmacology (having to do with neurotransmitters and related drugs). The Church provided most of our social opportunities, and actually I'm not sure that we ever had a formal "date" during our brief four months of courtship.
I really DID try to help Wayne with his pharmacology! Do you know how hard that is when you can't pronounce the words, let alone keep your mind on the subject? I will always be the cause of him not doing well in that subject! It could have been worse. It could have been surgery or some other subject!
Vicki comes from a wonderful family, and I don't think her father was too surprised when I formally asked him for his daughter's hand in marriage. The reality of what was happening struck me the hardest when Vicki showed me some drinking glasses she had in her little "dowry", with the monogram "AA" etched in them. "Wait a minute", I thought. "That's my initial!" It made everything seem a little final, and I was beginning to realize that there was no turning back now. That made me just a little nervous, but I think I overcame it as we began to make wedding plans.
Wayne never did officially propose to me! We knew we wanted to get married and I guess I wasn't a stickler about those kinds of things. I was really excited when he gave me a diamond ring though. I wasn't sure I would get one since he never really proposed! I remember buying something for our wedding trousseau and as a bonus I could order a set of glasses with any initial I wanted on them! I thought this was a chance to start our collection of things we would need when we got married. So I ordered a set of glasses with an "AA" on them. I thought that was neat because that made it more real!
Prior to our marriage, Vicki had an appointment with Dr. Hodges, a less-active member of the Church who was an obstetrician, for her pre-marital examination. He told Vicki that he wanted to talk to the two of us afterwards to tell us the importance of not having children for a least two years ("so you can get to know each other before the children come along"), but we had to rush off to a funeral where I had been asked to be a pall-bearer, so I never got the lecture. The result of that was the birth of Jonathan, ten months after we were married. We have never regretted that.
Wayne and I had had many talks about how many children we wanted. There was never any talk about when we would start our family. I think we both were thinking that we wanted our family without any delays! It really didn't matter what Dr. Hodges had to say because we had our own ideas of what we wanted for ourselves! I was quite surprised that as a member of the church (even though he was less active) he was counseling us to wait for a couple of years. We had even talked at one point about having 12 children! What were we thinking? (With the in-law children we have our 12!)
On Christmas day our parents saw us off at the airport, and we flew out to Salt Lake City, then took a bus up to Logan (the Salt Lake temple was closed), where we stayed with a family Vicki had known when they had lived in the Silver Spring Ward in Maryland (The Serge Benson Family).
We were married two days later, December 27, 1968, in the Logan temple, in a "double ceremony" with Jean Blana and her fiancé, (George Parks) whom we had known from the Washington Ward. Vicki's father had made arrangements for us to stay at the Hotel Utah, overlooking the Christmas lights on Temple Square, and we took a side trip to Park City, almost getting trapped in a blizzard while we were there. A good friend from the Washington Ward, who had moved back to Salt Lake City, loaned us her car for our one-week honeymoon in Salt Lake.
I remember we had reserved the "Honeymoon Suite". The surprising thing was that the wallpaper was peeling down in one corner of the room. We even took a picture of me trying to hold it up! It was a great room though, with a great view of Temple Square. It was beautiful as the snow fell and covered everything so pretty and white. And the lights were beautiful on Temple Square as well.
Back home, we settled into our first home, a small apartment on Greenwood Street in Takoma Park. I rode my motorscooter into D.C. to medical school, and Vicki drove the Volkswagen, which my father had helped us obtain, to her job as a secretary for a small accounting firm (O'Connell and Jorg) in Silver Spring. As alluded to earlier, she became pregnant about a month after we were married, and made frequent trips from her desk in the front of their office to the restroom in the back, where she emptied her stomach.
We kept a scrapbook of our first few years of marriage, but much of it was destroyed by some hungry mice. We also have lots of pictures (mostly crammed in boxes) and some movies. Now, nearly 29 years later, our fondest memories are of the times we have spent with our children, and we have enjoyed watching them go through their own courtships and marriages, and take great pleasure in seeing them begin their own families.

Question:

*I've inherited a box full of photographs and newspaper clippings
from my ancestors. The problem is that the items aren't
labeled in any sort of way. How can I start my family history
research when I have so many unanswered questions?*

I know exactly how you feel and have a personal experience to share. In
my family history box, I discovered a newspaper article about American
Indians. I wasn't sure why my grandfather had clipped and saved the article, but it lead me down a fascinating path of research.

Guess what? After asking family members a few questions and doing some
research on the Internet, I discovered that I might have some Cherokee
blood in my family line. What a fascinating aspect of my family history!

When you feel as though you have more questions than answers, it's true
that your research might feel overwhelming. However, I encourage you to
use those questions as starting points for gathering information about
your family connections. It's a great way to gather information you may
have otherwise missed.

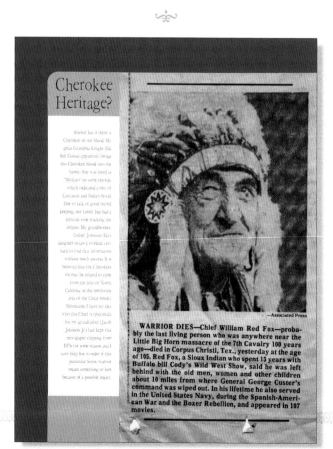

Checklist

We've probably all come across mysterious old photographs in our collections. The best way to identify the people in those photos is to ask other family members for information. Start with these questions:

1. What do you know about the photograph?

2. Do you know when the photograph was taken?

3. Do you know the people in the photograph?

4. Can you identify any details in the photograph (style of clothing, type of car)?

5. Do you know where the photograph was taken?

6. Who do you think the photographer might have been?

7. Do you have any similar photographs in your personal collection?

8. What does this photograph represent to you?

9. What sort of feeling and/or emotion do you connect with this photograph?

10. Does this photograph remind you of a special person, place or event in your life?

Question:

*How do I handle original scrapbooks and old journals?
Should I take them apart and re-do them?
How can I safely preserve them?*

This is a tricky question. At one point, I felt like I should remove photographs from old scrapbooks and preserve them with archival methods. But then I started thinking … in 50 years, do I really want someone taking my scrapbooks apart? My answer was no.

It's important to be respectful of the men and women in your family who took the time to scrapbook your family pictures. To preserve their hard work, consider taking photographs of each page in the albums and printing them out. You can also carefully scan old pages and photographs without causing any damage to the original pictures.

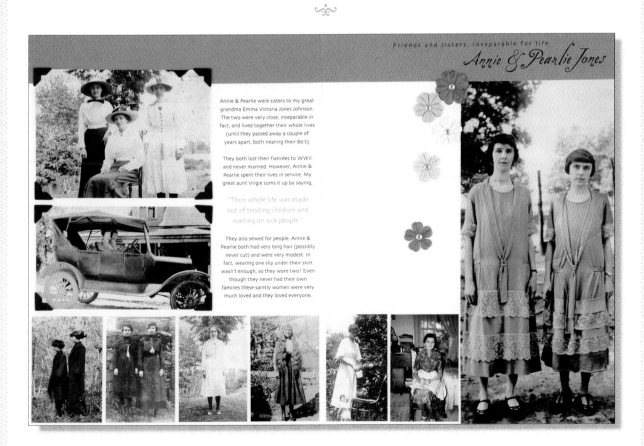

Friends and sisters, inseparable for life

Annie & Pearlie Jones

Annie & Pearlie were sisters to my great grandma Emma Victoria Jones Johnson. The two were very close, inseparable in fact, and lived together their whole lives (until they passed away a couple of years apart, both nearing their 80's).

They both lost their fiancées to WWII and never married. However, Annie & Pearlie spent their lives in service. My great aunt Virgie sums it up by saying,

"Their whole life was made out of tending children and waiting on sick people."

They also sewed for people. Annie & Pearlie both had very long hair (possibly never cut) and were very modest. In fact, wearing one slip under their skirt wasn't enough, so they wore two! Even though they never had their own families these saintly women were very much loved and they loved everyone.

DISCOVERING HISTORICAL FACTS

Question:

*How can I find information on what happened
the year my mother was born?*

The Internet is a wealth of information—you can find all sorts of historical facts and figures. My mom was born in 1948. I used Google to search for information on her birth year. Really, it was as simple as typing "1948" into the Google search engine.

Karen and I both used information we found on the Internet to enhance the journaling on our scrapbook pages here.

For a list of specific websites with historical information, check out the list on page 75 in Chapter 3.

The year that Edwin Hubble announced the existence of other galaxies. The US elects its first female governor. The *New Yorker* publishes its first issue. The Chrysler Corporation is founded. The Grand Ole' Opry makes its radio debut. New York City becomes the largest City in the world. First patent for the color television. The Santa Barbara earthquake destroys downtown Santa Barbara, CA. Scotch tape is invented. Calvin Coolidge becomes the first President of the US to have his inauguration broadcasted on the radio.

the year my Grandfather was born.

1925

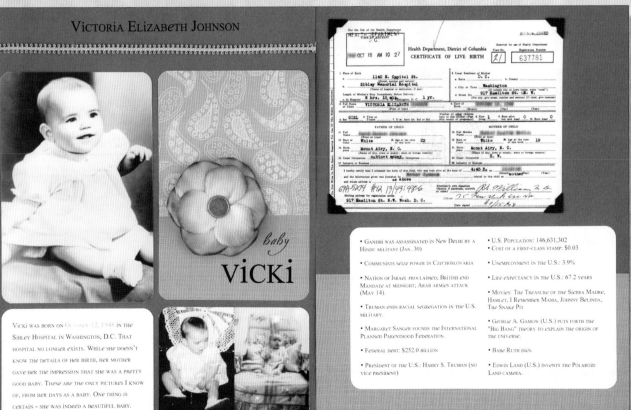

VICTORIA ELIZABETH JOHNSON

baby

ViCKi

VICKI WAS BORN ON October 12, 1948 IN THE SIBLEY HOSPITAL IN WASHINGTON, D.C. THAT HOSPITAL NO LONGER EXISTS. WHILE SHE DOESN'T KNOW THE DETAILS OF HER BIRTH, HER MOTHER GAVE HER THE IMPRESSION THAT SHE WAS A PRETTY GOOD BABY. THESE ARE THE ONLY PICTURES I KNOW OF, FROM HER DAYS AS A BABY. ONE THING IS CERTAIN – SHE WAS INDEED A BEAUTIFUL BABY.

- GANDHI WAS ASSASSINATED IN NEW DELHI BY A HINDU MILITANT (JAN. 30)
- COMMUNISTS SEIZE POWER IN CZECHOSLOVAKIA
- NATION OF ISRAEL PROCLAIMED; BRITISH END MANDATE AT MIDNIGHT; ARAB ARMIES ATTACK (MAY 14).
- TRUMAN ENDS RACIAL SEGREGATION IN THE U.S. MILITARY.
- MARGARET SANGER FOUNDS THE INTERNATIONAL PLANNED PARENTHOOD FEDERATION.
- FEDERAL DEBT: $252.0 BILLION
- PRESIDENT OF THE U.S.: HARRY S. TRUMAN (NO VICE PRESIDENT)

- U.S. POPULATION: 146,631,302
- COST OF A FIRST-CLASS STAMP: $0.03
- UNEMPLOYMENT IN THE U.S.: 3.9%
- LIFE EXPECTANCY IN THE U.S.: 67.2 YEARS
- MOVIES: THE TREASURE OF THE SIERRA MADRE, HAMLET, I REMEMBER MAMA, JOHNNY BELINDA, THE SNAKE PIT
- GEORGE A. GAMOW (U.S.) PUTS FORTH THE "BIG BANG" THEORY TO EXPLAIN THE ORIGIN OF THE UNIVERSE.
- BABE RUTH DIES.
- EDWIN LAND (U.S.) INVENTS THE POLAROID LAND CAMERA.

{
Question:

*Do you have any more tips on how to
conduct an effective interview?*
}

This is such an important topic that I've touched on it a couple of times in this chapter. Remember to keep the interview process fun and to conduct interviews in person when possible.

Another great technique is to bring photographs and memorabilia to your interview. An actual snapshot or document can help start the conversation rolling. Who knows what stories the pin Grandma wore at her wedding or a photograph of Grandpa's first car might elicit?

I also like the "tell me more" strategy. For example, I wanted to learn more about my father-in-law's experiences camping. I had heard that he encountered a bear on one particular trip. Instead of asking him, "Did you see a bear?" I used the approach of asking open-ended questions, such as, "Tell me lots of details, like how you pitched a tent and where you slept." One simple prompt is often all it takes to learn an awesome story.

Bear Encounter ... Sort of.

When I graduated from high school, I joined a few of my fellow graduates in the mountains to celebrate. We were going to drive up and go fishing and be on our own for a week or so. We loaded my brother's van and drove up to my uncle's little trailer home at Lake Luna, near Alpine, AZ. We stayed up there a few days and the fishing wasn't real good, so we decided to go up and do a little bit of stream fishing on the Black River, located west of Alpine in the White Mountains.

We drove down near this area and recognized a friend of ours, another guy from our high school. He was working with a Forest Service fire crew up there to clear brush. We asked him where we could find a good fishing spot and he directly us to "Wildcat Point". So we followed a trail and got to the point where we decided to camp. We pitched a tent by stretching a tarp from the open doors at back of the van to a limb then draped to the ground. Then dinner was quickly made in skillets on the campfire.

I brought a mattress to sleep on in the back of the van, and two friends placed their bedrolls under the tarp. As we were lying there and joking with each other, one of my friends suddenly shushed us because he thought he heard something walking. Quiet and listening intently, we heard nothing. So we began talking again and my friend, once again, thought he heard something. Listening again, we heard a growling sound.

We had no idea what it was. More than anything it sounded like a dog's growl or something. We didn't think it was a mountain lion. It was kind of funny. Before, we had met a guy downstream that said he had seen a gorilla. He was asking if there were any gorillas in these mountains. We were really hee-hawing that up – 'This guy thinks there are gorillas out here!' But by the time we heard all that growling, we were wondering if there were gorillas out here too!

We all heard the slow footsteps of the something getting closer. Its plodding sound was too loud to be a dog or something of the sort. We thought that it might be a bear, but it didn't really sound like a bear. So my friends quickly jumped in the back of the truck we me. We couldn't see out of the back window because we had set up the tent hitched to the back of the truck. We could only see out of the front windows. But with that view, nothing could be seen. Somehow we managed to sleep in the truck that night.

Before the daylight the next morning, we heard it come back again. When the sun rose, we loaded up our gear in the back and took off back to the lake. On our way out, we ran into their schoolmate again and told him their story. Old Gerry said, "Oh, I forgot to tell you guys, we've had some bear reports in that area." It looks like we had had ourselves a bear visit! It was quite an experience.

Checklist

1. As a child, what was your favorite movie?

2. Did you have family chores? What were they?

3. Did you receive an allowance? If so, how much?

4. What was your favorite subject in school?

5. Who was your favorite teacher and why?

6. What school activities and sports did you participate in?

7. What were the popular fashions when you grew up?

8. What were your favorite songs and music?

9. Did you have any pets?

10. What was your religion growing up? What church, if any, did you attend?

Question:

How do I access information, photographs and documents that are in the possession of another family member?

Old family photographs and documents are treasured items, and the people holding them for safe-keeping likely feel a sense of responsibility for them. It's true—those old items simply can't be duplicated if they're lost! Here are some strategies for accessing them:

* If you live in the same town, set up a time when you can meet at a local copy store and make copies of the originals.

* Own a scanner? Bring a scanner and a laptop to her home and scan originals.

* Bring your camera to her home and take pictures of original items.

* Borrow items in batches, scan them and give them back in a timely manner.

* Offer to share the results of your family history research and presentation.

P.E. in 1936

P.E. and granddaughter, Esther Jane Carlson (approximately 1918)

P.E. in Yorkville, IL 1923

Born in 1848, died in 1944 at the age of 96

P.E. Croushorn

Mahonri
The Poet

My Western Home

Oh, land of sunshine, land so free,
The dearest spot on earth, to me;
The place where first I came to earth,
Where sainted mother gave me birth;
To thee with pride I fondly cling,
Tho far away at times I roam,
I love thee still, my western home!

Oh, western land, so dear to me,
I love to breathe thine air so free;
From out thy mountains stored with snow,
Pure rippling, sparkling waters flow
Out on the fruitful, fertile plains,
Where fragrant flowers ever bloom,
And orange blossoms add perfume.

I love thy mountains rough and high,
Thy atmosphere so pure and dry;
I love thy valleys, hills and plains,
Thy winter snow and summer rains;
'Tis not for gain I plight my love,
But for the home thou gavest me,
I will in turn be true to thee!

Friends Old and New

The friends I make on life's highway,
Are dear to me today;
But they should never come before
The friends of yesterday.
If these prove true as those of yore,
Then I'm rich ever-more.

E'en tho I make friends by the score,
Whose lives enrich my store,
And lose the friends of yesterday,
I still am lean and poor.
May friends of yore and friends today,
E'er be my friends alway.

I fondly hope, with man – my friend –
In this New Year, to send,
A friendly message to mankind;
And be to all a friend.
Lord, may I in this service find,
Increased faith in all mankind.

Christ is Risen

Christ arose on Easter Morn,

Triumphant o'er the tomb

And brought to earth light and hope,

Dispelling doubt and gloom.

Opening wide the prison doors,

He set the prisoners free;

These are they once held in chains,

Now loosed eternally!

PIONEERS

Poems

BY

M. A. STEWART

Mahonri was a poet and this is *a collection* of some of his poems that we are blessed to have.

UNION POSTALE UNIVERSELLE

Scrapbooking Family Secrets

{ Question:

*What should I do if I stumble across "family secrets"
as I'm gathering information? How can
I handle the information in a sensitive way?* }

First of all, remember this: all families have secrets. People make mistakes and learn from them. Even though we like to think our relatives were perfect, they made mistakes just like we do.

Second, try and keep a sense of humor when possible. And don't take the secrets to heart. You don't have to live with their secrets, but perhaps you can learn something from what they experienced.

As you create your layouts, remember that you can use hidden journaling to conceal sensitive information. You can also create a "family secrets" layout or keep the information in a separate and non-public album.

information is tucked in pocket

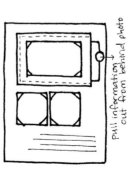

Pull information out from behind photo

lift pages to reveal information (sew or use brads to secure top of page)

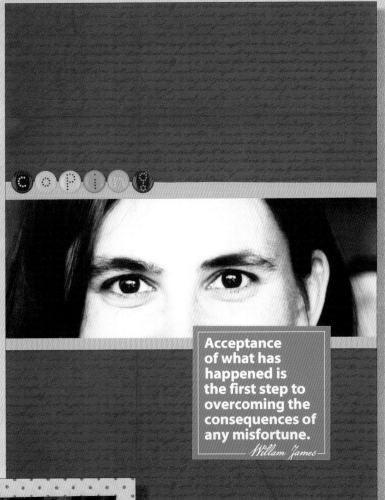

copies

Acceptance of what has happened is the first step to overcoming the consequences of any misfortune.
William James

t   m

1977

almost sisters
TANYA & MISSY

*M*y mother-in-law had a number of secret-coded love letters tucked away in an envelope that her grandmother and grandfather had written to each other in the early 1900s. My mother-in-law decided she wanted to feature them in an album as a gift for her 91-year-old mother. Together, she and I followed these steps to complete the album in just a couple of weeks:

1. GATHER. We gathered the letters and photographs of my mother-in-law's grandparents.

2. SORT. We sorted through the letters and made a list of which ones we wanted to include in the album.

3. PREPARE/ORGANIZE. We purchased supplies for the project at our local scrapbook store.

4. DISCOVER. We worked together to decode some of the letters that hadn't been decoded.

5. PRESENT. The finished album includes a title page, an introduction page, a sample code page, 10 featured letters, a page that stores other letters and six photo pages.

—Mimi Schramm

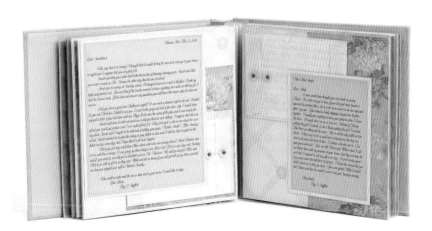

Victoria Elizabeth Johnson Allgaier
(your grandmother)

I want family history to be fun for my children, so I came up with two family history games we can play together as they grow.

The *first* game uses a set of flashcards. Each card has two sides—one side has a picture of a relative and the other side has a story or experience from that relative's life. I laminated the cards at my local copy store and then rounded the corners of each card. To play, we pick a card and read the story or experience. Then we try to guess which relative we're talking about. To find out the answer, we flip to see their picture on the other side. When we're not using them, the cards are stored in a plastic photo case from Cropper Hopper.

The *second* game is a card-matching or memory game using childhood photographs of my husband and me. First I cut a 12" x 12" sheet of patterned paper into 2" x 3" blocks. I reduced the photos to 2" x 3", placed the paper and photos back to back, laminated them at a copy store, then punched a hole in the corner of each card. This helps keep them together when we're not playing. Each card has a matching pair (two copies of the same photograph). To play this matching game, we simply place the cards face-down on a table and turn them over, one at a time, until we find matching pairs. The person who has the most matched pairs at the end of the game wins!

Use this worksheet to help you start your family history project. It will guide you toward the materials and documents you need to gather.

1. What sort of family history project do you want to create?

2. What time span do you want your family history to cover?

3. Which family members will read/view your family history album?

4. Will your album be focused on a certain person, couple or family?

5. What is your mission for your family history project?

6. Think about the photographs and documents you'll need to complete your family history project. What do have, what do you need to gather, and where can you find the documents you need?

Emma and me

June 1977
Becky is 8 months

August 1979
Emma's 100th birthday

You've created a family history corner in your home. Everything's in one place, and of course you celebrate this great accomplishment with a root beer float and a chick flick. But then, it's back to work. That was only the beginning, my friend. Now it's time to have some fun. And for those of you who love to organize (I know you're out there), you are going to love this part.

I know, I know. Those of us who get a thrill out of creating order out of chaos are a little less common than the I-wish-I-could-pay-someone-to-do-this type of people. But take a deep breath and don't even think about that option. This is your privilege to go through all the family history stuff you have and start sorting it into categories.

There is a helpful acronym in the organizing culture that I've referred to time and time again. It's from Julie Morgenstern, a professional organizer. Julie suggests that you organize in this order: Sort, Purge, Assign, Containerize and Equalize. That spells SPACE. But for the purpose of organizing family history materials, we're only focusing on the "S" right now.

Sort first. Don't start making random pages, and do not—I repeat—DO NOT throw anything away!

Sorting first brings clarity to the big picture and allows you to really gain an understanding of what you have and what you don't. If you came across a couple of pictures of your parents' wedding day and made that layout before sorting, you'll be very frustrated when you come across that one fabulous picture you didn't know about and didn't have to use on the layout.

So Julie, if you're out there, thank you. And should you ever be in Arizona and want to stop by for some organizational fun, call me (I'm not kidding!).

BECKY'S SYSTEM

Question:
*Becky, how do you sort
your family history information?*

After I've gathered everything into my family history corner, I start sorting through photographs and documents. At the beginning of the process, I like to sort information by family or by person. It's really easy for me to do and takes much of the frustration and guesswork out of my family history projects.

{
Question:
*I have so much information that I can't even decide
where to start the sorting process. Help!*
}

From talking with readers about family history, I understand
how overwhelming and frustrating it can be to have so much
information that you don't know where to begin. The good news
is that this step in the process—the sorting step—is going
to help you gain control over what might seem to be a tangled
and disorganized mess. My first piece of advice is to choose a
method for sorting your photographs. Do you want to sort by
family member, by timeline, by family story? Choose a method
and before you know it, you'll start seeing your project take on
an order.

As you sort through your information, you'll also be able to assess
what you have and determine what you need to track down. For
example, maybe you'll see that you have lots of photographs but are
unsure of the stories behind them. Or, you could have the reverse
situation. Perhaps you know several family legends, but you don't
have any photographs to illustrate those oral histories.

{ **Question:**
*How do I decide how I should
sort my information?* }

Choose an approach that feels comfortable to you. Research the family stories that are the most interesting, touching, heartwarming, engaging, motivating and/or inspiring to you. By working on research you love, you'll stay passionate about working on your family history (and your final results will definitely show it!). Plus, as you sort through your photographs and documents, you'll start seeing common threads that tie your family history information together. At that point, you'll be able to decide what approach you want to take on your scrapbook pages.

One approach is the informational approach. On the page at right about my great-great-grandfather, I included various bits of information about his life. Another approach is a story-based approach, such as focusing on stories and anecdotes, like the layout at right of my husband's great-grandfather. Ideally, try to use both approaches in your family history.

Adolf August Allgaier

Birth date: 31 Jan 1857

Birth place: Kankakee, Illinois

Parents: John Allgaier & Verena Brunner

Born & raised in Kankakee, the second of three children. His mother raised the children alone.

Marriage date: 2 Mar 1882 at age 24

Marriage place: Kankaee, Illinois

Spouse: Sarah Hansing (age 18 at time of wedding)

Children:
Emory Leonard
Roy Dwayne (my great grandfather)
Irvin Eugene
Mabel Carrie

Widowed at a young age. Baby Mabel lived for only 4 months & Sarah died 4 days later of the same disease – tuberculosis. This left Adolf with his 3 sons (ages 4, 6, and 9) to raise on his own.

Death: 4 Sept 1916 (age 59)

Death place: Bradley, Illinois

Death cause: pernicious anemia

Burial place: Salina Township, Kankakee, Illinois

Known employment:
Servant in the C. Sexton Household (a nurseryman & his wife) – age 23

Day laborer when married – age 24

Worked for Len Small (who later became the governor of Illinois) in Kankakee

Rented a farm with his brother, Emil, and they raised Perceron draft horses

Homesteaded near his 2 sons in northwestern South Dakota

Health was failing him so he moved back to Illinois
Farmer at time of death, according to death certificate

(1857 – 1916)

In his own words: Stories from Lorenzo's Childhood

SCARRED FOR LIFE

On the last day of school one year I had taken mother's little 4-inch penknife and was cutting my initials in the side of a hickory tree. The penknife slipped and I **cut my left thumb** (right corner) and all these years it has left a mark and my thumbnail splits there.

CREATIVE HIDING PLACE

When I was around three or four years old the neighbor women came over to visit mother and I was so shy I crawled **under mother's skirts** and played with her garters.

SURPRISE ENCOUNTER

During my school days there was a little hollow tree that had a bird's nest in it. I pulled eggs out one at a time and broke them and then pulled the nest out in pieces. Then I pulled and pulled on something that wouldn't come up. I discovered I had a **snakehead** in my hand and I let it go in a hurry and it popped back into the tree stump and I ran as fast as I could.

THINK TWICE

Once when I took cattle back to the pastures when I was a kid I saw a **hornet's nest**. I threw a clod at it. A hornet came out of it so fast, like a bullet and hit me right between the eyes and threw me to the ground. I let hornet's nests alone after that.

{ **Question:**
*I have so many documents—I don't know
which ones I should keep and which ones I should
throw away. Please help me decide!* }

It can be hard to judge what's important! I suggest keeping anything that's hand-written (like checkbook registers and old love letters) as well as anything that helps tell your family stories or that gives you special insight into a family member's education, career, lifestyle or personality. This layout, for instance, displays my grandfather's old report cards. These records showed me how he performed as a student and gave me a glimpse into history (how fun it was to see which classes he took!).

As far as throwing stuff away? Well, that's a difficult call to make. Check with relatives before you decide to toss anything (remember, if someone saved it, he or she may have had an important reason for doing so). The checklist at right will give you some ideas on what to do with those extra items.

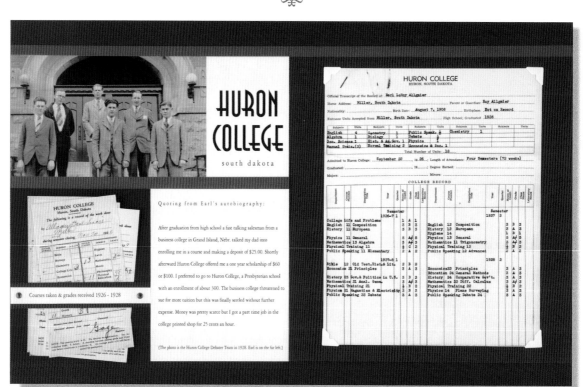

Checklist

EXTRA PHOTOGRAPHS AND MEMORABILIA

What can you do with the extra photographs and memorabilia you don't use on your current projects? Here are a few ideas:

1. Share the items with other family members who may be interested in incorporating the memorabilia into their projects.

2. Sort the extra items into categories, photograph them as groups, then scrapbook those photographs.

3. Slip extra photographs into photo sleeves and store them in a binder.

4. File old documents in an acid-free box.

5. Label binders and boxes with the surname of the person/family in your ancestry.

6. Store your extra memorabilia in a dark closet and away from any heat and/or water sources.

7. Use extra photographs in a creative way, such as in a family history game.

8. Incorporate photographs into home-decor projects.

9. Create single pages for your current scrapbook.

10. Photocopy items for your children to use for history and geography projects for school.

❋

❋

❋

SCRAPBOOKING MEMORABILIA

Question:

*What should I do with letters, cards,
certificates, property deeds, bills and other kinds
of memorabilia and documents?*

These items are important because they give such an authentic
glimpse into history and into the lives of the people you're
scrapbooking. When I find items like these, I sort them into
the appropriate person's folder. Once I assess what I have, I
scan the items, resize them, print them out and include them
on my scrapbook pages.

It's true that you can include original documents on your
scrapbook pages, but I really do suggest using scans whenever
you can. One-of-a-kind documents like birth certificates,
marriage licenses and especially letters (which can never
be recreated if they're lost) should be stored in a place like
a family safe.

Wedding Day

EARL & ESTHER ALLGAIER

MR. WESLEY KOSIN, PASTOR OF THE LITTLE PRESBYTERIAN CHURCH THEY ATTENDED, PERFORMED THE CEREMONY. THEY HAD A WEDDING BREAKFAST FOR 12 AND JUST AS THEY STARTED THE CUCKOO CLOCK CHIMED 12 NOON, WHICH EVERYONE FOUND TO BE PRETTY FUNNY. THE NEWLYWED COUPLE LEFT FOR THEIR HONEYMOON IN EARL'S 1931 MODEL A FORD, WITH CANS TIED ON THE BACK AND "JUST MARRIED" WRITTEN ALL OVER IT, THANKS TO ESTHER'S BROTHERS.

EARL & ESTHER WERE MARRIED AT THE CARLSON HOME NEAR YORKVILLE, ILLINOIS ON AUGUST 24TH (1938) AT 11:00AM. EARL HAD A PROBLEM WITH SOME OF HIS TEETH AND HAD TO GO TO THE DENTIST THAT MORNING AROUND 9:00. HE BARELY GOT BACK IN TIME FOR THE WEDDING. WITH A SENSE OF HUMOR, EARL COMMENTED THAT "THE WEDDING KISS FELL ON LIPS DEADENED WITH NOVACAINE!"

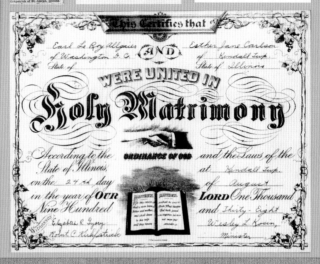

Earl's resume' in 1932

Earl's resume' in 1942

{ **Question:**
*As I sort my items, how do I know if
they're safe to include in a scrapbook? Or how do
I make them safe to put in a scrapbook?* }

When I got my hands on my grandma's documents and memorabilia, I realized I had a lot of random stuff. I had a ton of appointment cards and receipts, so I preserved just a few using deacidification spray, which can deacidify anything as long as you cover the document evenly. This doesn't restore yellow documents to their original state, but it stops the deterioration process by neutralizing acid content. Make sure to either scan or deacidify all of your old documents; if use untreated originals, acid can spread through your scrapbooks, destroying your hard work and memories!

On my layout here, I included quite a bit of memorabilia but kept it separate from the photographs on my page. If you're ever using documents that haven't been treated, make sure to keep the documents separate from your photographs. Otherwise, acid could spread from the documents to your photographs and destroy them.

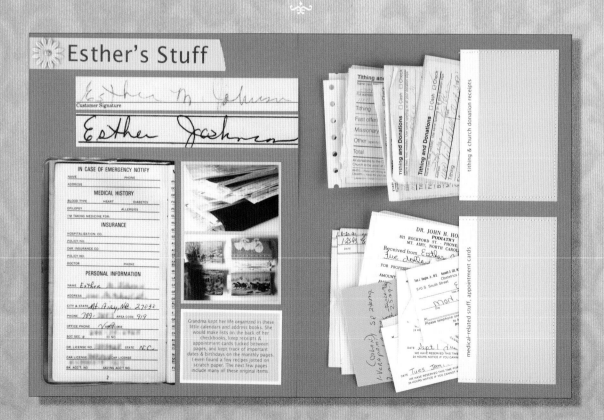

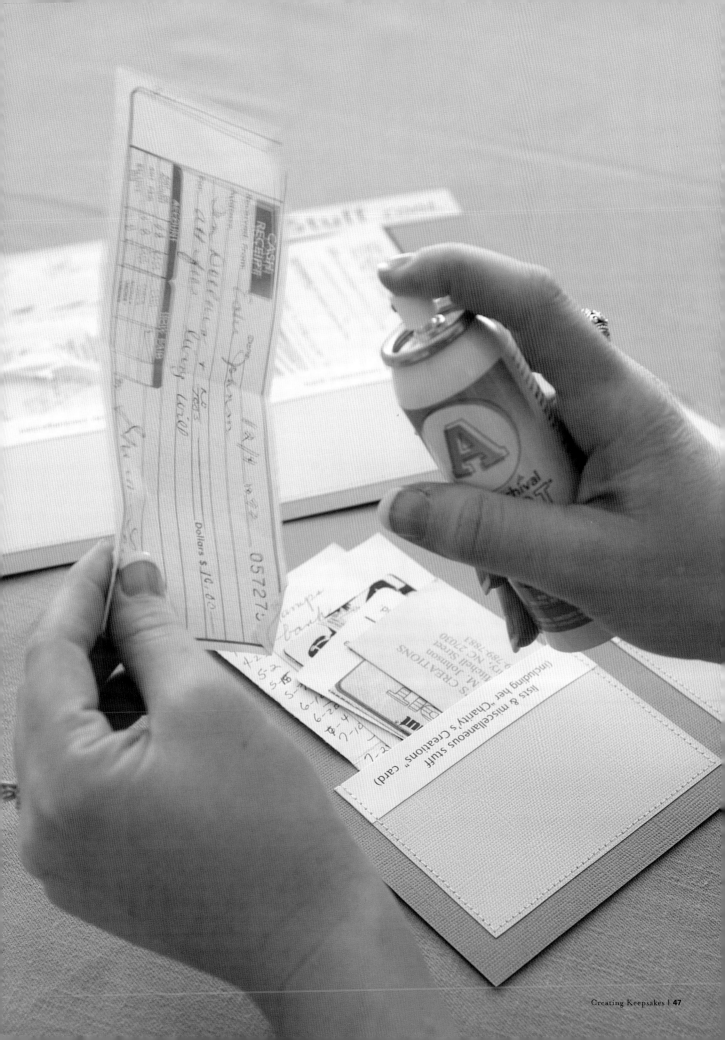

Question:

What should I do with medals, pins, medallions and other bulky objects that are important to me? Do I have to scrapbook them all, or do I have other choices?

Photograph bulky items using straight shots. When I photographed my dad's high school letter for the layout below, I stood above it and took a straight-on shot. A straight shot is important because it helps create an accurate representation of the item. A crooked shot may give an item a distorted look and feel.

You'll find more tips on how to photograph bulky items on page 78 in Chapter 3.

the
letter

Getting a letter was COOL. Wayne, like many others at Washington Lee High School, proudly wore his letter on his v-neck, button-up sweater. You earned this by being in high school sports for all 3 years of high school (10th, 11th, 12th grades). The small emblems represent the specific sports in which you were involved. Wayne's wrestling emblem is shown here. He's not sure what the bar is for – perhaps an extra year in that sport?

Why do I have a small collection of pigs?

Grandma's PIGS

Because my grandma had a LARGE collection of pigs. I am not sure why she collected pigs, but I think they just made her happy. We always joked that we were going to buy her one of those giant cement lawn ornament pigs and have it dropped off in her yard. Maybe that is why she moved into an apartment...she knew we were goofy enought to do it. When she passed away, I did not want to take the entire collection. My aunt took most of them, but I took a few to remember her by. It is odd how the little things define us.

{ **Question:**
*I want to create a layout around a family tree.
How do I go about it?* }

The Internet has hundreds of websites with family tree documents that you can print out and use as starting points for collecting your family information. Just type "family tree" into your favorite Internet search engine and you'll pull up all kinds of forms. One site I particularly like is About Genealogy *(http://genealogy.about.com)*.

You can also use your creativity (like Rachel Ludwig did on her page at right) and design a family tree that fits your unique family history. If you want to use photographs on your family tree, it's important to scan and resize them first. Your family tree will look much nicer if you crop all of your photographs to a single size. I did this with my friend Tina's pictures on the layout at right and the end result is clean and orderly.

Tina Lynn WHITE

Marvin George WHITE

Susan SUTHERLAND

George Alton WHITE

Ruth McFARLAND

Gordon Henry SUTHERLAND

Leda JOHNSON

George Dennis WHITE

Alice C. GUNN

Arch McFARLAND

Drucilla HOLMES

Henry SUTHERLAND

Mildred BENSON

Palmer JOHNSON

Bertha RAWLINS

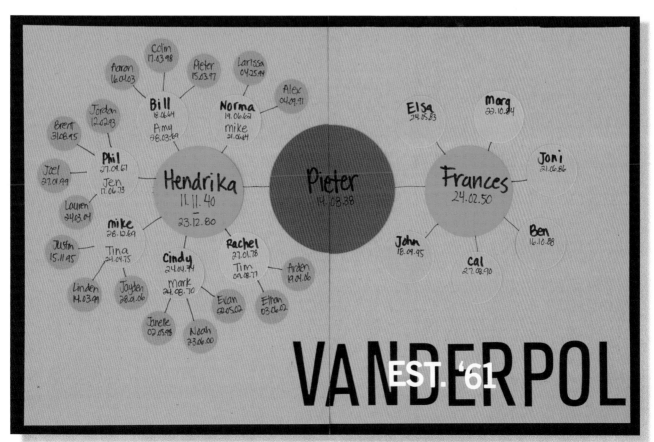

SCRAPBOOKING LETTERS

Question:

I have tons of letters that family members have written to each other, but I'm struggling with how to sort and scrapbook them. What should I do?

You should consider yourself lucky if you have this problem! Letters are a virtual gold mine of information. Letters give you an inside look into the habits and personalities of your family members. Plus, letters are often full of historical references that will help you understand the time in which your family members lived.

If you have letters, take them out of their envelopes. Then unfold them and sort them into sheet protectors. Be sure to save the envelopes too—with their addresses, postage stamps and old postmarks, they're another priceless source of information. Place the envelopes in sheet protectors as well.

As for scrapbooking letters, take a look at my "Love Letters" layout at right. Instead of photocopying the letters to use on my page (which is perfectly acceptable and fine to do), I scanned the letters and envelopes and printed the images. Scanning preserves their authenticity, yellowing, tears and all.

Love Letters

These are copies of letters from Earl to Esther written a couple of years before their marriage. This newspaper clipping to the right ("I love you") has a handwritten note on the back that Esther wrote before sending this to Earl: "I cut this out of the Pathfinder in 1929."

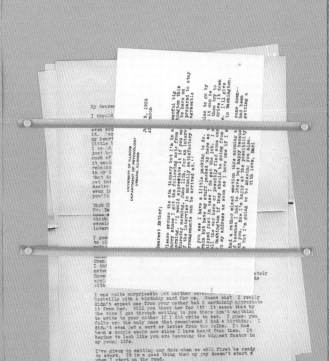

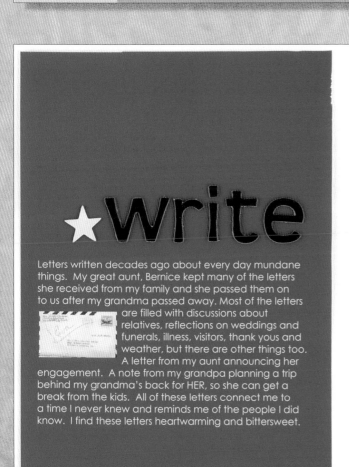

★write

Letters written decades ago about every day mundane things. My great aunt, Bernice kept many of the letters she received from my family and she passed them on to us after my grandma passed away. Most of the letters are filled with discussions about relatives, reflections on weddings and funerals, illness, visitors, thank yous and weather, but there are other things too. A letter from my aunt announcing her engagement. A note from my grandpa planning a trip behind my grandma's back for HER, so she can get a break from the kids. All of these letters connect me to a time I never knew and reminds me of the people I did know. I find these letters heartwarming and bittersweet.

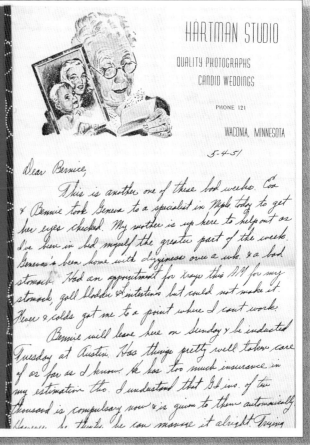

Question:

*I have so many old photographs—how
should I begin to sort them
into "scrapbookable" categories?*

The answer really depends on what you want to accomplish with your family history projects. I suggest going through your photographs and deciding which ones help you share the story you want to tell or make you curious about your family history. It's important to remember that you're not under any obligation to scrapbook every single family photograph you inherit! You can always save the photographs you don't scrapbook in photo-safe sheet protectors and/or boxes. And, you can also share duplicate photographs with other family members.

Checklist

10 Ways to Sort Your Photographs

Have a huge box of unsorted photographs and don't know where to start? The good news is that there are many different approaches you can take to sorting your photographs. Below is a list of 10 helpful options. Choose the method that works best for you and the story you want to tell.

1. Sort by family and/or by individual.

2. Sort by date (by month, year, decade, etc.).

3. Sort by photo size and type (Polaroid? 3" x 5"? 8" x 10"?).

4. Sort by event (Christmas, Halloween).

5. Sort by photo color (sepia, black and white, color).

6. Sort by location (home, work, school).

7. Sort by life event (graduation, wedding, new baby, birthday).

8. Sort by clothing styles.

9. Sort by travel and/or vacation.

10. Sort by known and unknown.

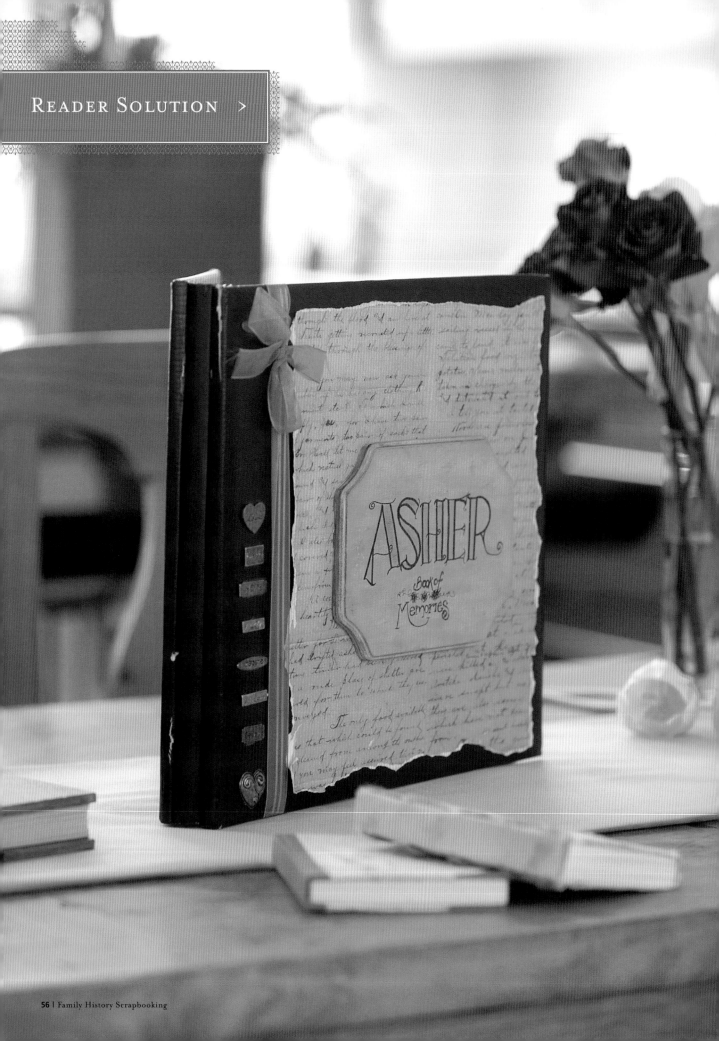

*I*n late 1990, my grandmother was diagnosed with cancer. She's been in and out of remission for years, and my grandfather has done little else but take care of her every need while continuing to play an integral role in the lives of his children, grandchildren and great-grandchildren.

Last year, I thought it would be really meaningful for my grandparents to receive a gift from my entire family, and my concept for the "Asher Book of Memories" was born. I sent invitations to all of my family members, asking them to bring photographs and memorabilia to a four-hour crop at my house. I was thrilled to have over 30 family members between the ages of two and 50 show up and work on scrapbook pages for my grandparents' gift.

Here's how we followed the five-step process outlined in this book to complete their special album:

1. GATHER. Each family member gathered up his or her favorite old photographs.

2. SORT. We set up long tables and shared stories and photographs as we sorted through the boxes of materials to choose the pictures we each wanted to scrapbook.

3. PREPARE/ORGANIZE. I set up scrapbooking stations so each family member could easily choose the supplies he or she needed to complete a page.

4. DISCOVER. Because we worked on this project as a family group of 30 people, we were able to help

answer each other's questions as we talked about the photographs.

5. PRESENT. It took us four hours to complete the project. I created the album cover and title page, and we gave the completed album to my grandparents as a gift.

—Jen Lehmann

Include your progenitors in your everyday life by featuring them in your home decor. It's a great reminder of where you came from and will teach your children about their roots. For my family history collage, I chose to feature couples and marriages, but you can choose any theme you'd like.

To create your collage, first choose your pictures. I found great shots of my parents, my husband David's parents, and all of our grandparents. You'll want to scan the photos so you can make them whatever size you want.

The next step is to run to your local Target (I love you, Target) or the store of your choice for frames. You may even have some frames around the house that will work well. Choose a variety of sizes. I kept my overall look simple (black) to really emphasize the pictures and because, well, that's just my style. Choose a clock, a shelf, anything else you want to add.

Print your photos to size and slip them in the frames. Next, arrange your pieces on the floor until your collage looks right. Then trace each piece (the clock, the frames, etc.) on tissue paper. (I actually used packing paper because I just moved and had a ton of it around!)

The next step is to mark where your nails should go and then lightly tape your pieces of paper on the wall. Then hammer the nails right through the paper. Remove the paper, hang your pictures and othe elements, and step back and take a look at what you created! Nicely done.

Use this worksheet to help you sort through the photographs and documents you want to use for your family history project.

1. Think again about the scope of your project and jot it down here.

_____

_____

_____

2. How many photographs do you think you'll need (take a guess!) to complete your project?

_____

_____

_____

3. How will you sort your photographs?

_____

_____

_____

4. What kinds of documents will you use for your project?

_____

_____

_____

5. How will your sort your documents?

_____

_____

_____

6. What will you do with your extra photographs and documents?

_____

_____

_____

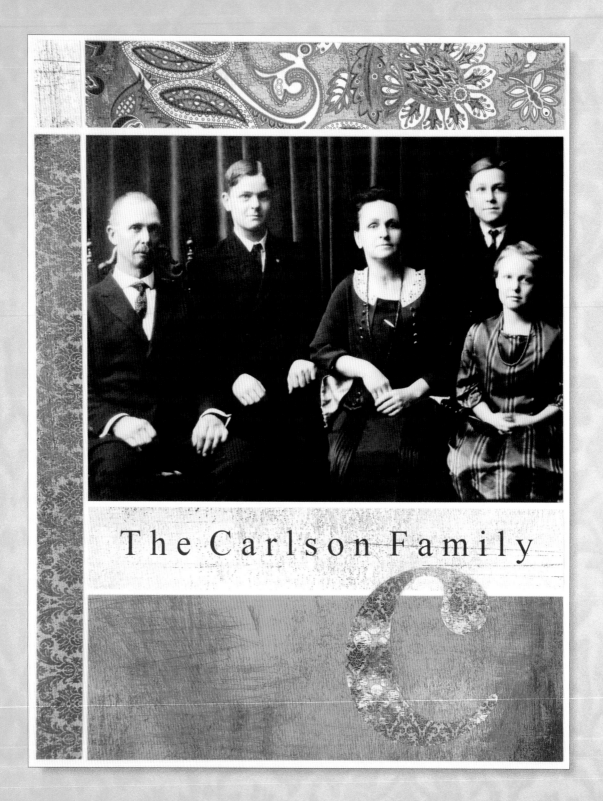

The Carlson Family

Have you ever painted a room in your home? If you have, you know how important it is to prepare the room before you even pick up a paintbrush! I know it can take hours to clean the walls, tape off the baseboards and ceiling, remove outlet covers and so on, but it's well worth the time. You make fewer mistakes. The carpets stay clean. And when you're done? The room looks great, and you're happy you took the time to do the job right.

Painting, family history … it's all the same. Preparing is part of the big picture. And even though preparation takes time, you'll be happy to know that this step will actually help you feel less overwhelmed by the family history process.

In this chapter, I encourage you to take the time to choose an organization system and get prepared before you start the process of scrapbooking your family history. I'll share my favorite organizational tips and ideas, but remember—these are just the methods that work for me.

Ultimately, do what works for you! It's important to tell your family stories in a way that makes sense for you.

So let's talk about it. Let's talk about negatives and photo restoration and what to do about missing information, and what to do with large items that don't fit in scrapbooks. I'm sure if I were sitting there with you, we'd get off on a lot of tangents, but for now, let's prepare and organize. Stay focused, my friend. We're getting there!

BECKY'S SYSTEM

{
Question:
*Becky, how do you organize your
family history information?*
}

As I mentioned in Chapter 1, I've created a wonderfully
simple solution that works well for me: I have a binder
for each family, and each binder includes a section for each
person in that family. I also have a list of topics to scrapbook for each family and/or family member. This makes it
easy to access my information and allows me to work on
pages from different "books" when I have time.

{ **Question:**
How can I preserve old negatives? }

As I was researching my family history, I was thrilled to come across my parents' wedding negatives. (Yes, Mom, I promise to give them back!). With my handy-dandy scanner, the Epson Perfection 4490, I scanned the negatives into my computer and printed them as photographs. I'm delighted with the end results—the photos are beautiful!

When I first scanned the negatives, I noticed that the colors weren't as sharp as they could be. My photo-editing program allowed me to easily fix the colors and print out the photographs you see on this layout.

Based on my personal experience, my advice is to scan your negatives and then store the originals in negative protectors. (Check and see if your scanner has the ability to scan negatives and/or slides. If not, check with your local photo store and see if they have a scanner with this capability.) You can buy sheet protectors for negatives at any photo supply store.

Wedding Reception

Wayne & Vicki were married on December 27, 1968 in the Logan Temple. Because they traveled so far for the wedding, and NO one was able to be there with them, they had their wedding reception two weeks after the wedding, in January. It was held in the Silver Spring Stake Center where Vicki's family went to church (Silver Spring Ward).

Deep purple and lavender were the obvious choice of colors for the bride. Purple has always been Vicki's favorite color. The reception was rather large with a lot of people from both sides of the river; Virginia for Wayne's family and friends and Maryland for Vicki's family and friends.

*Vicki and Wayne
December 27, 1968*

{ **Question:**
I'm not sure which organizational system is best for me. Can you give me some different options I might try? }

You can organize your family history information in a variety of ways. Start with what you have and look for common denominators that will help you organize your information into groups. For example, I like to scrapbook by family, by couple and by individual person. Within each of these sections are topics (like my grand-parents' love story, as shown on the layout at right, which goes in the "Earl & Esther" section).

Perhaps you'd like to organize your information chrono-logically (for example, by year or by decade). Another useful approach is to start with a list of topics you might want to scrapbook for your family. A few topics that are important to me are education, career, life roles, church service and relationships.

A hint? Choose a system before you get too far along in the process; you'll save yourself hours of frustration wondering where to keep your photographs and docu-ments. You'll also be able to add new information as you receive it. And, if you have people in your family helping you with your project, you can easily explain your organizational system to them, making it easier for them to pitch in.

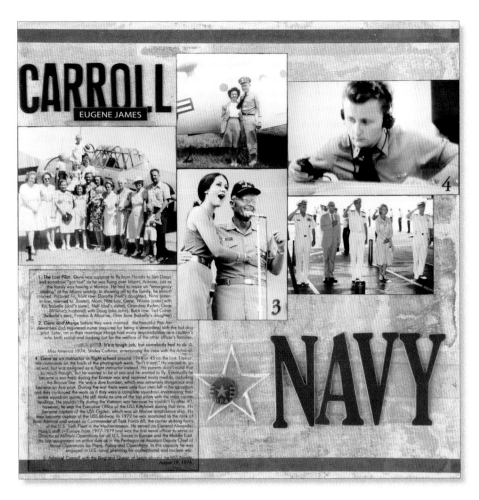

CARROLL
EUGENE JAMES

NAVY

1. The Lost Pilot. Gene was suppose to fly from Florida to San Diego and somehow "got lost" as he was flying over Miami, Arizona, just as the family was having a reunion. He had to make an "emergency landing" at the Miami airstrip. In showing off to the family, he almost crashed. Pictured is... front row: Dorothy (Nell's daughter), Nina (sister-in-law, married to Buster), Mom, Nita Lou, Gene, Winnie (sister) with Kit, Isabelle (dad's sister), Nell (dad's sister), Grandma Ryden, Gene (Winnie's husband) with Doug (aka John). Back row: Ted Culver (Isabelle's son), Frankie & Maurine, Ellen Jane (Isabelle's daughter)

2. Gene and Marge before they were married... the beautiful Pan American stewardess and registered nurse (required for being a stewardess) with the hot dog pilot. Later, on in their marriage Marge had many responsibilities as a captain's wife—both social and looking out for the welfare of the other officer's families.

3. It's a tough job, but somebody had to do it. Miss America 1974, Shirley Cothran, entertaining the crew with the Admiral.

4. Gene as an instructor in flight school around 1944 or 45 on the Link Trainer. His comments on the back of the photograph were, "Isn't it sad". He wanted to go to war, but was assigned as a flight instructor instead. His parents didn't mind that so much though, but he wanted to be at sea and he wanted to fly. Eventually he became a war-hero during the Korean war and received many medals, including the Bronze Star. He was a dive bomber, which was extremely dangerous and became an Ace pilot. During the war there were only four men left in his squadron and they continued the work as if they were a complete squadron-maintaining their entire squadron quota. He still ranks as one of the top pilots with the most carrier landings. He couldn't fly during the Vietnam war because he couldn't fly after 40, however, he was the Executive Office of the USS Kittyhawk during that time. He became captain of the USS Ogden, which was an Marine amphibious ship. He then became captain of the USS Midway. In 1972 he was promoted to the rank of Rear Admiral and served as Commander of Task Force 60, the carrier striking force of the U.S. Sixth Fleet in the Mediterranean. He served on General Alexander Haig's staff in Europe from 1977-1979 and was the first naval officer to serve as Director of Military Operations for all U.S. forces in Europe and the Middle East. His last assignment on active duty of in the Pentagon as Assistant Deputy Chief of Naval Operations for Plans, Policy and Operations. In this capacity he was engaged in U.S. naval planning for conventional and nuclear war.

5. Admiral Carroll with the Bags and Orders of State at ... of the USS Nimitz. August 19, 1976.

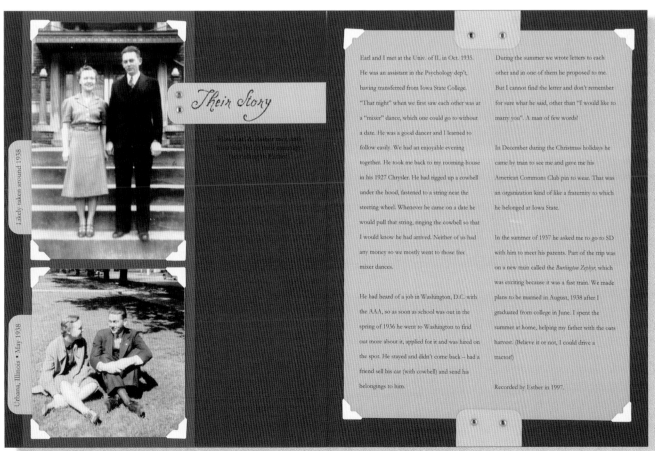

Likely taken around 1938

Urbana, Illinois • May 1938

Their Story

How Earl & Esther met, and how they led to their marriage
(according to Esther)

Earl and I met at the Univ. of IL in Oct. 1935. He was an assistant in the Psychology dep't, having transferred from Iowa State College. "That night" when we first saw each other was at a "mixer" dance, which one could go to without a date. He was a good dancer and I learned to follow easily. We had an enjoyable evening together. He took me back to my rooming-house in his 1927 Chrysler. He had rigged up a cowbell under the hood, fastened to a string near the steering wheel. Whenever he came on a date he would pull that string, tinging the cowbell so that I would know he had arrived. Neither of us had any money so we mostly went to those free mixer dances.

He had heard of a job in Washington, D.C. with the AAA, so as soon as school was out in the spring of 1936 he went to Washington to find out more about it, applied for it and was hired on the spot. He stayed and didn't come back — had a friend sell his car (with cowbell) and send his belongings to him.

During the summer we wrote letters to each other and in one of them he proposed to me. But I cannot find the letter and don't remember for sure what he said, other than "I would like to marry you". A man of few words!

In December during the Christmas holidays he came by train to see me and gave me his American Commons Club pin to wear. That was an organization kind of like a fraternity to which he belonged at Iowa State.

In the summer of 1937 he asked me to go to SD with him to meet his parents. Part of the trip was on a new train called the *Burlington Zephyr*, which was exciting because it was a fast train. We made plans to be married in August, 1938 after I graduated from college in June. I spent the summer at home, helping my father with the oats harvest. (Believe it or not, I could drive a tractor!)

Recorded by Esther in 1997.

Question:

Should my family history scrapbooks contain only old photographs, or should I include new photographs as well?

First, these are your family history scrapbooks, and you should scrapbook your stories in a way that feels right for you and your family. However, I think it's wonderful to create a link between past and present by pairing older family pictures with photographs you've taken today. For example, my mom had a special pair of white gloves when she was a young woman. I photographed the gloves to use on a layout that shows pictures of her actually wearing the gloves.

You can also create a wonderful layout by taking pictures of buildings, places, colleges, churches and so on and pairing them with older pictures of the same exact places. It's a great way to show how things change and stay the same over time.

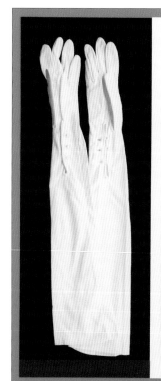

pretty
as a
princess

The Event

The Deputante Ball was a (church) stake event where young women that reach the age of 16 are "presented" by their fathers. It was held at the Mexican Embassy in D.C. Her first dance was with her father, followed by an entire evening of dancing. These 3 photos were taken before & during that event. The above left photo is Vicki, escorted by her father. The above right photo is her dancing with her brother Jacob.

The Gloves

Vicki loved these long, fancy white gloves and bought them herself just to go with her dress. (Her mother made the dress, just as she made a lot of Vicki's clothes.) This was her first and only pair of long gloves. The only other time she remembers wearing them was for some stake dance (shown on the left page). She recalls that her date for that evening was a tall, blonde twin from the College Park Ward in their stake.

Vicki turned 16 in 1965.

Checklist

Comparing historic photos with current ones is a terrific way to give your family history layouts a "then and now" perspective. It's easy, creative and, above all, fun! You'll see just how much times have changed in only one or two generations. Here are some ideas to get you started:

1. Pair a photograph of your grandmother's elementary school with a picture of your son's elementary school.

2. Pair a photograph of your mom doing research for a school project at the library with a picture of your daughter using the Internet to do research.

3. Pair a photograph of your grandfather's sports team with a picture of your son's sports team.

4. Pair a photograph of your grandmother's school class with a picture of your daughter's school class of the same grade.

5. Pair a photo from your prom with a photo from your daughter's prom.

6. Pair a photo of your mom listening to records with a photo of your daughter listening to her iPod.

7. Pair a photograph of your mom's first car with a photo of your daughter's first car.

8. Pair photographs of inside your grandparent's first home with photos inside your current home to show differences in decor and technology (TVs, computers, telephones, etc.).

9. Pair photos of your parents when they were teenagers with photos of your teenagers and even you as a teenager.

10. Research old photographs of sites in the city where your parents lived (local historical societies and old family photos are good resources). Then revisit these locations and re-photograph them. Display the old and new photos together on a scrapbook page.

FIXING DAMAGED PHOTOGRAPHS

Question:
How do I preserve the damaged
photographs I've received?

You can take a couple of different approaches for fixing those old photographs. I use my scanner and photo-editing software. When I found the old military photo on my layout at left, it had a red splotch on it. I simply scanned the photo, desaturated the image (making it black & white) and then added a little color for a sepia-toned effect. As you can see on my layout at right, this easy fix gave my old photograph new life.

If you have really old photographs, you might want to consult with an expert on photo retouching. An expert can touch up your original photographs and may be able to restore them to a near-original state. Look for "photo retouching" services in your local yellow pages, or consult the staff at your favorite local photo store for recommendations.

WWII

"Co. I. First N.C. Inf., Mt. Airy, N.C."

With this information, I still know nothing.

I don't know if I have an ancestor in this picture.

But I tend to think maybe it's *not* an ancestor I'm looking for.

This was found in Annie & Pearlie's scrapbooks with

no explanation, but one has to wonder if one of

their fiancés was in this infantry. Both of their fiancés

died in the war, so perhaps that is why the sisters saved this picture.

> Question:
>
> *I want to use snippets of information I've found in old journals, family Bibles, etc., on my pages. What's the best way to include this information in my scrapbook?*

Family Bibles and old journals are priceless caches of information about your family history. They're a wonderful starting place for discovering stories that might have otherwise been forgotten. My mom, for instance, came across an old hymn book with inscriptions inside. As I photographed the book and scanned the pages, I was excited to notice that I could read the names inscribed inside the front cover.

My mom discovered that one of the names was that of a missionary who taught her great-great-grandparents about a religion they ended up joining. Just imagine: from a single name in a book, my mom discovered the conversion story of her ancestors. She was also able to track down this missionary's family and learn even more about our family history.

I encourage you to use your family documents as starting points for your research. Remember that you can also scan pages that include handwritten names and family information. Reduce or enlarge the scans in size and include them on your scrapbook pages.

By the way, be sure to store journals, books, and other records in a safe place. This is a bookcase in our home that houses our family history records, albums, books, and journals. It's also where we keep love letters between my husband and me, which are preserved in a box that he made from scratch when we were first married. I love having it all in one place.

our
LDS Roots
in North Carolina

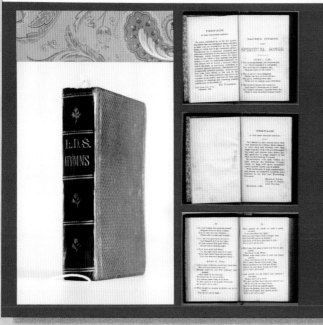

Our LDS Roots in North Carolina:
A 123-year Missionary Reunion
[1882 – 2005]

From the mountains of Utah to the hills of North Carolina and back

By Victoria Elizabeth Johnson Allgaier

April 7, 2004. At the urging of my family I am going to attempt to write some of my "discoveries" over the past few days, which I have found to be quite exciting. Let me begin by going back a number of years.

The first clue: Two little books with inscriptions

My Mother, Esther Chanty Marion Johnson, gave me two small books; one being a red book entitled *Missionary Song Book,* measuring 3" x 5". The inscription reads "Pearla M. Jones her song book. A present from Elder James A. Mortenson, this the 22nd of September 1901". The other book, being black and measuring 3" x 4 3/4", entitled *LDS Hymns* has an inscription which reads "Dr. James D. Dean, St. Paul, Carroll Co., VA From W.J. Millard, Farmington, Davis Co., Utah" with no date signed.

Who was baptized first in our family?

I want to share a very special experience regarding that little black book. Over the recent days I have wondered about the missionary who was instrumental in teaching the Gospel to my mother's side of the family. Who was the first in our family to be baptized and when were they baptized?

The beginning of my search: A phone call to Aunt Virgie

Wayne and I had watched General Conference on Saturday and Sunday, April 4th & 5th,

SHARING STORIES WITH NO PHOTOGRAPHS

{ **Question:**
*I have lots of family stories but no pictures
to illustrate them. What should I do?* }

First of all, it's wonderful that you have those family stories! Do your future generations a favor and take the time to record and scrapbook them before they're completely lost. You can take several approaches for sharing stories without photographs. Consider these options:

* Just write the story down. I created a page about my grandma's driving that doesn't include a photograph. As you can see on my layout at right, this story doesn't need an illustration!

* Download photographs from the Internet. On Joy's layout about her family of farmers, she illustrated the story with photographs of Philippine farming communities that she found online.

* Combine two photographs to tell one story. For example, if you're scrapbooking the story of how your great-grandparents met but don't have a picture of them as a couple, consider using a single photograph of each of them.

* Be creative! Look at high school yearbooks, brochures, postcards, newspaper clippings and more to find photographs to illustrate the stories you're sharing on your pages.

Learning to Drive

Esther's younger brother attempts to teach her

Although Wendell was two years younger than Esther, he attempted to teach her how to drive in Papa's (their father's) 1928 Chevrolet when they were kids. Across the dirt road from their home was a lumberyard. Their neighbor, Matt Hines (sp?), made shipping pallets from the lumber, so there was a lot of it stacked up in the field. According to Wendell, this was a great place to learn because there were no police, no other cars, and plenty of space. He tried to teach Esther how to change gears, work the clutch, etc. He's not sure if she actually learned much. Wendell remembers that she was not really "automotive inclined", as he calls it. Or maybe his patience just wore out, he tells me with a chuckle.

This story came out in a conversation I had with Wendell in April 2006.

FAMILY OF FARMERS

Being a first generation American, born in Chicago in the 70s, it is easy to forget that my grandparents, their parents and their parents' parents lived a life so unlike my own. Both sets of my grandparents were farmers back in the Philippines. Mom's family, the Cavidas of Lucban, Quezon on the island of Luzon, owned land on which they planted rice, coconuts, mangoes and other vegetables. Further north in Luzon the Fernandez family of Solano, Neva Vizcaya grew rice, coconuts, cabbage, tomatoes and other vegetables. Both sets of families farmed in order to provide sustinence and an income.

In order to cultivate the land, both families depended on caribous (water buffalos). No modern conveniences such as tractors. In fact, Kuya Rolly, who is my first cousin on the Cavida side and the only farmer among the cousins, still uses caribous on the farm. Having seen him plow in the rice fields with a caribou during a visit to the Philippines in 1988 when I was twelve - that is something I will never forget. We had taken a picture. I wish I knew where the picture was. I wish even more that I had a picture of my grandparents farming on their land.

Today, both sets of land has been divided between the children of my grandparents. My aunts and uncles and my parents. I hope that someday I will be able to take my children to these farms so that they can know and experience a little bit of our heritage, our history, our homeland.

Question:
*I have tons of pictures, but I'm missing
the stories behind them! Help, I have
no idea what to do next!*

Asking relatives about the photographs is a good starting point. If you can't find any information about your photos, however, you can always turn to the Internet and fill in the gaps with historic information. Start by examining your photographs for a detail you can research online. Maybe you'll notice some clothing or a street sign that might lead you down a fascinating path of research. A personal example? I came across these photographs of my grandpa's old car. I knew the Model A Ford was important to him, so I typed "Model A Ford" into my search engine and came across all sorts of interesting information about the car's history. You'll see that I incorporated that little history lesson onto this layout!

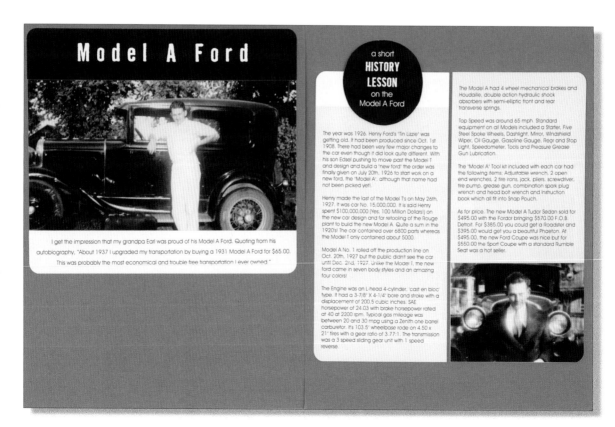

Model A Ford

I get the impression that my grandpa Earl was proud of his Model A Ford. Quoting from his autobiography, "About 1937 I upgraded my transportation by buying a 1931 Model A Ford for $65.00. This was probably the most economical and trouble free transportation I ever owned."

a short
**HISTORY
LESSON**
on the
Model A Ford

The year was 1926. Henry Ford's 'Tin Lizzie' was getting old. It had been produced since Oct. 1st 1908. There had been very few major changes to the car even though it did look quite different. With his son Edsel pushing to move past the Model T and design and build a 'new ford' the order was finally given on July 20th, 1926 to start work on a new ford, the 'Model A', although that name had not been picked yet.

Henry made the last of the Model Ts on May 26th, 1927. It was car No. 15,000,000. It is said Henry spent $100,000,000 (Yes, 100 Million Dollars!) on the new car design and for retooling of the Rouge plant to build the new Model A. Quite a sum in the 1920s! The car contained over 6800 parts whereas the Model T only contained about 5000.

Model A No. 1 rolled off the production line on Oct. 20th, 1927 but the public didn't see the car until Dec. 2nd, 1927. Unlike the Model T, the new ford came in seven body styles and an amazing four colors!

The Engine was an L-head 4-cylinder, 'cast en bloc' type. It had a 3-7/8" X 4-1/4" bore and stroke with a displacement of 200.5 cubic inches. SAE horsepower of 24.03 with brake horsepower rated at 40 at 2200 rpm. Typical gas mileage was between 20 and 30 mpg using a Zenith one barrel carburetor. It's 103.5" wheelbase rode on 4.50 x 21" tires with a gear ratio of 3.77:1. The transmission was a 3 speed sliding gear unit with 1 speed reverse.

The Model A had 4 wheel mechanical brakes and Houdaille, double action hydraulic shock absorbers with semi-elliptic front and rear transverse springs.

Top Speed was around 65 mph. Standard equipment on all Models included a Starter, Five Steel Spoke Wheels, Dashlight, Mirror, Windshield Wiper, Oil Gauge, Gasoline Gauge, Rear and Stop Light, Speedometer, Tools and Pressure Grease Gun Lubrication.

The 'Model A' Tool kit included with each car had the following items: Adjustable wrench, 2 open end wrenches, 2 tire irons, jack, pliers, screwdriver, tire pump, grease gun, combination spark plug wrench and head bolt wrench and instruction book which all fit into Snap Pouch.

As for price. The new Model A Tudor Sedan sold for $495.00 with the Fordor bringing $570.00 F.O.B. Detroit. For $385.00 you could get a Roadster and $395.00 would get you a beautiful Phaeton. At $495.00, the new Ford Coupe was nice but for $550.00 the Sport Coupe with a standard Rumble Seat was a hot seller.

Checklist

LINKS TO HISTORICAL FACTS AND FIGURES

Wondering what happened during a certain year in history and how it might have influenced the lives of your family members? Here are some online resources that will help you gather the facts and figures you need to help tell their stories.

1. Baby Boomers

   www.babyboomers.com

   Includes information for the years 1946–1964

2. Did You Know?

   www.didyouknow.cd/history

   Lists inventions, discoveries and happenings through the centuries

3. What Happened on Your Birthday?

   http://channels.netscape.com/atplay/birthday.jsp

   Lists happenings for the birth date you enter

4. Fact Monster

   http://www.factmonster.com/yearbyyear.html

   Includes facts from 1900–today

PREPARING LARGE DOCUMENTS

{
Question:
*What should I do with large documents
like certificates, photographs, etc.,
that won't fit into my scrapbook?*
}

You might not always want to include original documents
and papers in your scrapbooks. You can, however, easily
scan and resize those items to fit on your pages. As you'll
see here, I had access to a photo of my grandmother's
high school class. I scanned it and also cropped in on her
face because I wanted her to be the focal point of the page.

A rule of thumb? If it fits in your scanner, scan it! If it
doesn't fit, try photographing the item. And remember that
you can scan an item and then reduce it to fit on your page.
I like how Loni created a memorabilia pocket on her layout
at right, which holds copies of documents that she scanned,
reduced and printed.

Yorkville High School

i l l i n o i s

Class of 1933

Esther was one of 39 in her graduating class.

What Esther recalls about high school:

For 8th grade we were in the regular high school building on the first floor. All the rest of the grades were upstairs where we had a **large assembly room**, and went from there to our classes (it was like a home-room is today).

I made **a lot of friends** during those four years together in high school. There were 39 in my graduating class. I **sang for a couple of years** in the girls' glee club and accompanied them in my senior year. There were no clubs as they have today in the schools.

The only foreign language was **Latin**, which I took, and it was a very easy subject for me. We had the regular subjects such as algebra, geometry, chemistry, physics, English.

Elbert was 5 years older than I so he was not in high school with me, but David (3 years older) was a senior when I was a freshman. He played football, and **at the games** we stood on the sidelines and ran up and down following the plays. No bleachers.

When I was in 8th grade (7th too), Elbert was still in high school, and he drove a horse and buggy and left it with Mr. Almy who had a barn near the school. Margaret Murley who lived further away from town than we did also drove a horse and buggy and somewhere along the way to town we would meet and **have races** with each other.

After school when I came home it seemed like there was always the **ironing** to do, and I was taking **piano lessons** so I did a lot of practicing, too, which I enjoyed. No girls basketball teams. Not any dating going on, but did have one for the senior dance.

MEMORABILIA I'VE SAVED OVER THE YEARS, FROM FRIENDS & FAMILY. **WORDS & MOMENTS** THAT MEANT A LOT TO ME.

DOCUMENTS & PHOTOS *enclosed...* LIFT FLAP

{ *Question:*
Can you share some tips for photographing
items that won't otherwise fit in my scrapbooks? }

Here's a quick list of my strategies:

✳ Try to use natural light but not direct sunlight. Your
garage is a good place to shoot.

✳ Don't use a flash.

✳ Choose a simple black or white background to keep
the photos timeless.

✳ Make sure there are no kids or patio furniture in the
background of your photos.

✳ Add visual interest to your photos by shooting from
different angles.

**recipe
box**

Esther Jane Carlson
University of Illinois (1933 – 1938)

Esther studied Home Economics at
the University of Illinois, so it's no
wonder that she had this recipe box
from her college days. From what I
can tell she did a lot of cooking and
baking along with her studies. I'm
unsure about the box herself but it's
possible Earl made it for her. In any
case, the recipes are meticulously
organized and still in good shape.
The box even included a brief log of
handwritten notes, I imagine for one
of her assignments or projects.

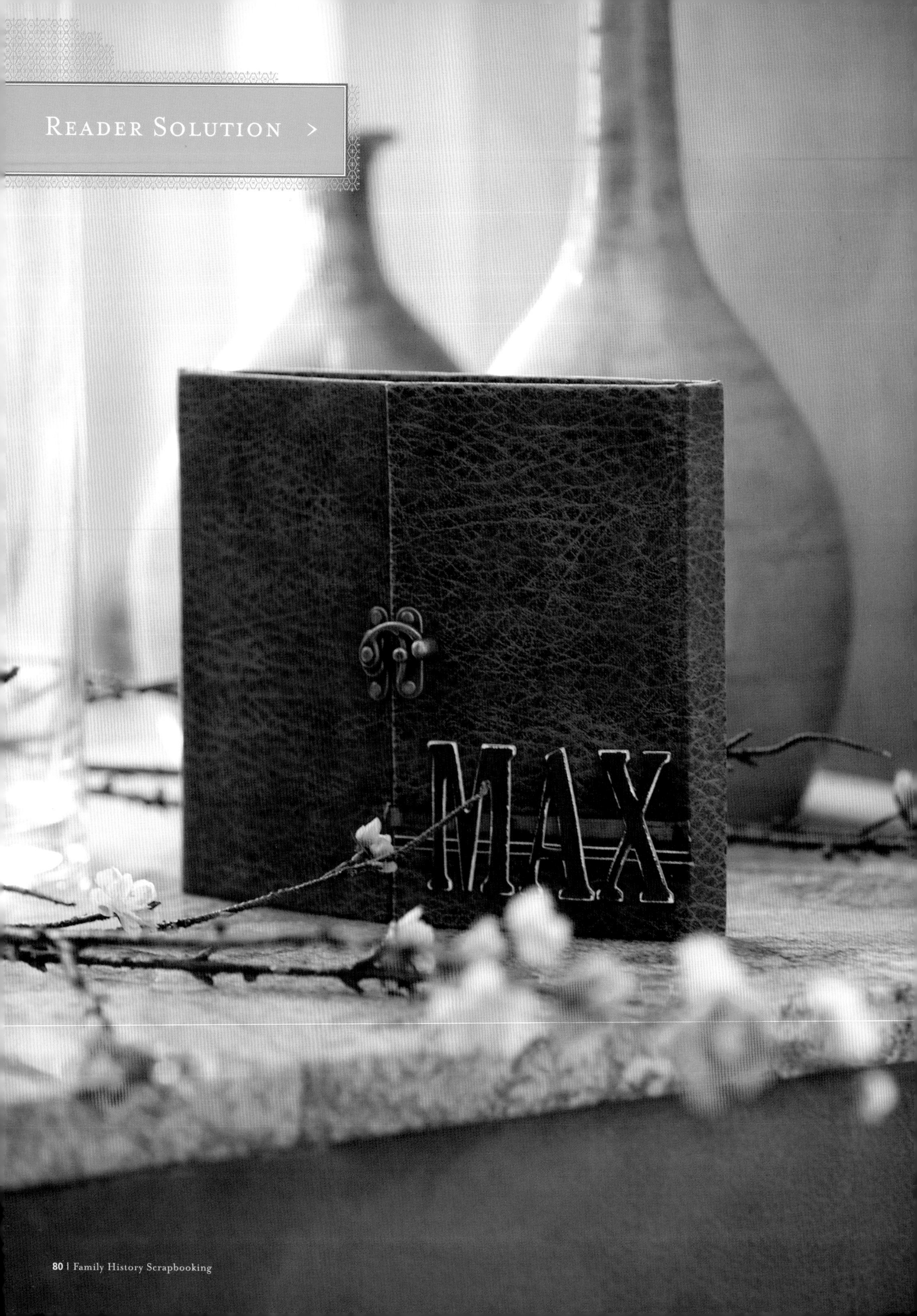
MAX

I created a birthday album for my dad as a surprise for his 70th birthday. I loved this project—it gave me the opportunity to create a special gift, and I learned so much about my father. Here are the steps I followed:

1. GATHER. I collected various photographs of my dad from important moments in his life.

2. SORT. As I looked through the photographs, I started seeing an obvious chronological pattern and began identifying how certain subjects went together.

3. PREPARE/ORGANIZE. I grouped the photographs into the following categories: youth, early family years, pastimes and hobbies, and current life.

4. DISCOVER. I was pleased to discover additional information on the back of some photographs, so I typed it up to include on my pages.

5. PRESENT. I used patterned paper from the same company to create a sense of unity throughout the album.

—*Kerri Bradford*

F amily history doesn't have to mean albums full of dates and names! I think it's fun to take a creative approach, especially when sharing family history with children.

I love to read to my kids, and I knew a family history storybook would be a fun way to have them become more familiar with their parents, grandparents and great-grandparents. I kept my pages simple in design and typed the words in a kid-friendly font. This little book fits easily into my children's hands and is a fun way to share our family connections.

You can easily create a family storybook for your children, nieces and nephews or grandchildren. Start with a topic and then create a template so you're repeating the information. You might also enjoy starting with your child's favorite childhood book and using the book as a starting point for your own family fairytale!

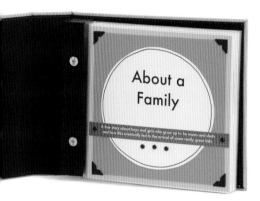

Use this worksheet to help you prepare and organize your family history.

1. What kind of organizational system will work best for you?

_____

_____

_____

2. What supplies do you need to organize your family history?

_____

_____

_____

3. What photographs or negatives do you have that need to be fixed?

_____

_____

4. What family documents do you have, and how will you scrapbook them?

_____

_____

5. Make a list of family treasures you want to photograph for your project.

_____

_____

_____

_____

_____

6. What information are you missing at this stage in the process?

_____

_____

I'm glad we have so many nice pictures of Grandma Allgaier (see row of photos below). She was a lovely woman. But it's pictures of her laughing and being silly that are absolutely delightful and really show

the fun side of Esther!

With so many serious and posed pictures in our family history, this is truly refreshing. We see and realize that our ancestors loved to laugh, have fun, and enjoy life just as we do. There were difficult times, but happy times as well.

Note from Becky (granddaughter): I believe this was taken in the early years of their home in Arlington, VA. Esther is sitting along the edge of their driveway, looking into the garage.

If you're already a scrapbooker, I hope you've found the joy of discovery in your hobby. Scrapbooking can help you realize more about yourself and your subjects (places, people, things in your life). Family history is discovery. It can be a journey that you never expected. You may learn things about your ancestors that are almost unbelievable. Some information may be hard to swallow. Some of what you learn may bring you to a greater sense of self.

This is all part of discovery. It's so much more than dates and facts and occupations and places of residence.

It's about having a greater realization of what your ancestors experienced, how they survived during difficult times, and what they did to stay strong. You will gain a greater appreciation for the life you have today. You'll learn to not take for granted the simple conveniences in life, like air conditioning, functioning cars, Super Target and disposable diapers.

You may even learn more about the health histories of your ancestors. This will help you know what you're prone to struggling with in your life. Take that information, share it with your doctor and take care of yourself.

Discovery is also about connections. It's about realizing that your quirks are similar to Grandpa's, and that your great-grandmother struggled with the same issues you did as a teenager. And who knew that your son's eyes are from your great uncle? Absorb it all. Keep a journal. Record your discoveries. Embrace your family's history and learn from it. Learn from your loved ones' examples as well as their mistakes.

The first step in discovery? Evaluate what you already know and then you'll know what you're looking for. Ready to get started? Here's how.

BECKY'S SYSTEM

Question:
*Becky, tell me more about
the discovery process you follow.*

For me, the discovery process is one of the most fascinating parts of family history. In doing family research, I've discovered interesting legends, found the missing puzzle pieces to family stories, stumbled across some sensitive information and have learned more about myself in the process. One of my favorite ways to share information is by chatting via web cam with my mom. It's a great way to share information with my whole family. I think the discovery process is a combination of talking with relatives and doing research on the Internet to fill in missing information. I also like to keep a list of unanswered questions on hand as I do my research because I've discovered that I sometimes find the answer to one question when I'm searching for the answer to a different question.

Question:

*How can I incorporate old
recipe cards into my scrapbooks?*

I absolutely love finding old recipes and incorporating them onto my scrapbook pages. You might find recipes that are neatly typed or handwritten on index cards (truly a treasure trove of information about what your family liked to eat, which can be a reflection on where they lived as well as their socio-economic status), or you might discover recipes written on random things, like slips of paper.

I recommend scanning or photocopying old recipe cards and then including the scans on your scrapbook pages. I also recommend making the recipes and sampling the results. You might just be surprised! A recipe from 1940 might not taste as good today—but perhaps there's a story behind the recipe about how Grandma also substituted a certain ingredient to make her cakes so delicious!

My mom made incredible desserts. Just looking through her recipe file brings back all sorts of memories—not to mention cravings! Peppermint Icebox Dessert was my favorite! I always asked for this for my birthday. Vanilla Pineapple Dessert was also something that I constantly begged for. I often would sneak in the kitchen and have some of the leftovers—and then get scolded for doing so. My mom also made the best Lemon Pie from scratch! No matter how much I'd try, even when I would do exactly as she had done, I could *never* make the crust as good as she could. It was incredible! This pie was a work of art and always in demand. I was never much of a pie eater, but with this one I definitely had to have my fair share. Then there's the Orange Mallow Sherbet that mom made often in the summer and was just a tasty treat. She always made her desserts from scratch with fresh ingredients. No one ever turned down an invitation to my mom's house for dinner. She was an incredible cook and was known for her trout, duck and turkey dinners. She knew how to cook and she enjoyed it.

Recipes from the files of Kathleen Ryden Carroll
Journaling 050606 by Anita Louise Carroll Bradford

RECIPES

{REMEMBER}
[REMEMBER]
1. TO BRING TO ONE'S MIND A
PAST EXPERIENCE. 2. NEVER FORGET.

just DESSERTS

handwritten RECIPES

Grandma Johnson loved collecting recipes. Whenever she learned of a new recipe, she would jot it down on whatever she had handy – inside her checkbook, on a piece of scrap paper, the back of a receipt, and sometimes she would actually write it on a recipe card. We don't know that she ever really kept all of her recipes in one place. No particular book or box contained all of her favorites. This is very telling of one of Esther's characteristics, which is that she wasn't the most organized person. But the woman could cook! I love seeing her scribbled notes and handwriting. I notice that when she prints (as opposed to writing cursive), she mixed upper and lower case letters. That was her signature handwriting.

{ **Question:**
I keep discovering receipts, brochures, pamphlets, programs and postcards in my stacks of family history documents. Any ideas on how to incorporate details from these items onto my pages? }

It's wonderful that you have these items in your possession! There are all kinds of great ways to include them on your scrapbook pages. As always, I suggest scanning or photocopying old documents whenever possible, like the birthday trinkets from my great-grandmother's life on my layout at right. But after that, the sky's the limit. Here are a few ideas to help you get started:

✳ Combine old postcards of a favorite family vacation spot with new postcards. Imagine how cool it would be to create a layout that showcases your family's vacations to a certain beach or amusement park.

✳ Create a travel album centered around the vacation postcards you discover in your family history box.

✳ Photocopy the front and back of postcards so the handwritten inscriptions can be enjoyed just as much as the postmarks, stamps and postcard pictures.

✳ See if you can find photographs that match the postcards, brochures and other documents in your collection. For example, if you have a play program, see if you can find pictures of your relatives attending the play.

✳ Use receipts, brochures and postcards as important clues into your family's daily lives. A collection of receipts, for instance, will show you where they shopped and how they chose to spend their money. Even a simple grocery store receipt can provide fascinating insight into their past.

EMMA CARLSON

BIRTHDAY
Girl

Mrs. Carlson Has 85th Anniversary

Miss Mary T. Howell — 553-3981

Na-au-say.—One of the outstanding social events of the late summer was the celebration of Mrs. Emma Carlson's 85th birthday anniversary.

Her children, Dr. Elbert Carlson of Genoa, David Carlson of Yorkville and Mrs. Earl (Esther) Allgaier of Arlington, Virginia, with their families, arranged an open house in her honor, held Sunday afternoon and evening in the David Carlsons home.

Mrs. Carlson, in a becoming dress, wearing an orchid corsage, with her family, smilingly greeted her guests, arriving from far and near. The perfect summer afternoon was an ideal setting for the stream of relatives and friends coming to offer their congratulations to a friend of long acquaintance. The afternoon was not only a time of expressing good wishes but also an opportunity for old friends to meet old friends.

Mrs. Carlson, alert and gracious, looked for everyone's comfort, as she chatted with groups in the various rooms. She was the recipient of many cards and gifts. Her two granddaughters, Mary Carlson and June Allgaier, had charge of the guest book, in which 85 or more signed their names. Refreshments were served from an attractive table by attentive members of the family.

It was memorable occasion, closing with the oft repeated "Many more happy birthdays!"

Emma had a lot of birthdays — **one hundred** of them, to be exact. Esther (Emma's daughter) seemed to enjoy having little birthday celebrations for her mother and these pictures are from those occasions. I imagine Esther always made the cake herself. I'm not sure who the other women are with Emma (seated in the middle) of the left page, but the picture at left below was taken on her 84th birthday. Picture at right – not sure which year. This note was signed by U.S. President and Mrs. Ford in 1976 and the newspaper article was written for her 85th birthday in 1964.

Warmest congratulations on your birthday. Our sincere wish to you on this special day is that the blessings of health and happiness may be yours in the years to come.

Betty Ford   Gerald R. Ford

Aug. 1976

Thelma was daddy's little girl, his firstborn. Raised in Tennessee, she moved with the family to Detroit during the Depression, but her heart remained back home in the South. World War II hit her hard, when several brothers and her childhood sweetheart Sterling were shipped out overseas to participate in the Allied effort. During a military leave, Thelma and Sterling slipped away and got married. Her daddy Richard was heartbroken.

"Are you too mad at me? I hope not, Daddy dear…"

He shouldn't have worried, for his little girl was in good hands. Sterling announced the first time he set eyes on six-year-old Thelma (he was ten) walking up the hill on her first day of school that she was the girl he was going to marry. After their elopement in Nashville, they took a bus to Bates Hill and strolled, under the stars, singing and holding hands, to his parents' home. Two days later he returned to the front.

At his wife's funeral in 1981, Sterling leaned over the casket just as it was closed for the last time, kissed Thelma's forehead, and whispered, "I'll see you on the other side, little girl." Grandpa Richard, Aunt Thelma, and Uncle Sterling are all gone now, but their story will always be a cherished part of our family history.

prodigal

THIS SPACE FOR WRITING MESSAGES

POST CARD

JOURNALING WITH PERSONAL MEMORIES

Question:

*I didn't really know my great-grandparents
and only have faint memories of meeting them a few times
when I was a child. How can I best tell their story?*

Most of us don't know our great-grandparents. In fact, mine had passed away before I was born, and I have to say that I don't have any memories of them. I do, however, have friends who have faint memories of their family members. I encourage those friends to write down what they do remember.

Journaling about those personal memories—even if they're limited in scope—is an important way to record your thoughts and impressions about family members. Set aside a couple of hours to recall those memories and to let your mind wander back to meeting them. A friend of mine remembers meeting her great-grandfather and how he smelled like pipe smoke and how he owned a talking parrot who sat on this shoulder. And how he rode his bike around town wherever he went!

Take a peek at how my friends Sabrina and Lisa journaled about their family members based on what they did know about them. I think you'll find that their pages are authentic, real and definitely worthwhile, even if they aren't packed with detailed information.

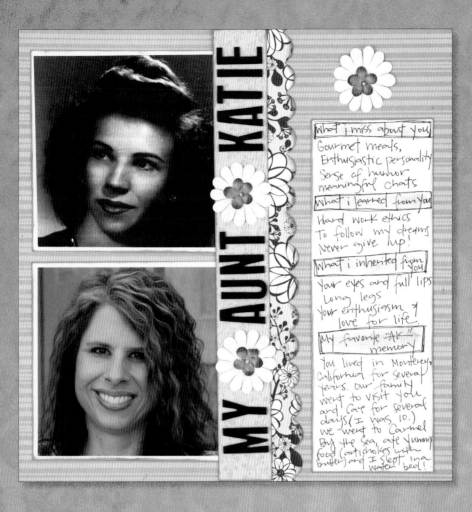

MY AUNT KATIE

What i miss about you
Gourmet meals,
Enthusiastic personality
Sense of humor
meaningful chats

What i learned from you
Hard work ethics
To follow my dreams
Never give up!

What i inherited from you
Your eyes and full lips
Long legs
Your enthusiasm &
love for life.

My favorite "AK"
memory
You lived in Monterey,
California for several
years. Our family
went to visit you
and Caye for several
days (I was 10.)
We went to Carmel
by the Sea, ate Yummy
food (artichokes with
butter) and I slept in a
water bed!

Memories of Grandpa

He worked wonders with **wood** - I always liked visiting him because he made these paddles out of wood and we would use them to play a mini baseball game. He always had wood toys to play with. Most of his fingers on his left hand were just stubs because he cut them off while working with wood. It didn't stop him from doing what he loved, though.

I will always remember the time he taught me to **color** inside the lines. He would show me how to do it, hand a crayon to me, and then watch me as I tried to mimic him. He painted some great pictures and I'm so glad he passed some of his ability on to me.

1993

To this day, whenever I see **maple nut ice cream** I think of him. It was his favorite and he always had some when my family visited.

Grandpa was **always whistling** Except his whistle was soft and sounded like the wind coming through a small crack in a window. I loved hearing it and made it a point to master his whistle.

He was a great **gardener** - especially loved picking fresh raspberries off the bushes at his house. I also remember the taste of the peas he grew; they were so fresh and crisp. It will never leave my memory that for breakfasts he and grandma would always give us apricot juice that he and grandma had canned. He also grew the best tomatoes in which he would sprinkle sugar on a freshly cut one and eat it. He ate his cottage cheese with sugar as well.

August 1983

I will always remember him and grandma standing in the driveway, **waving goodbye** to us as we drove away. Sometimes when we were almost to the end of the street, I would turn around and they would still be standing there watching us go.

1995

{

Question:

In researching my family history, I've stumbled across sensitive documents, like photographs taken at funerals and death certificates. Should I scrapbook these documents and death-related photos, and how?

}

Photographs of caskets and newspaper obituaries aren't exactly cheerful subjects to scrapbook—but most of us do have sensitive information in our family history collections, and we need a respectful way to scrapbook these items. Here are a few of the ideas I've used:

✳ Hide the photos. Create hidden photo pockets on your layouts where you can tuck photocopies or scans but still access them. Take a look at how I've used hidden pockets on my layout at right for casket photos of my great-grandmother.

✳ Keep it basic. I slipped a death certificate into a plain sheet protector for display.

✳ Design simple pages. You don't need (or probably want) to create heavily embellished and/or artistic pages about death. Simple, respectful pages can be the best in this situation.

The End of Emma Marion's Life

In the Spring of 1944 Emma became quite ill and went to see the doctor. They ended up performing emergency surgery on her, where they discovered her colon practically destroyed by cancer, which had also gotten to part of her liver. They weren't even sure she would survive the surgery, but she went home and lived for 9 more months.

It was inevitable that the cancer would eventually take her life so she went to stay with her parents and sisters (Annie & Pearlie) so they could care for her. Meanwhile, John (her husband) and Virgie (her oldest daughter) took care of the rest of her family. Virgie's husband, Troy, was away in the service so she was able to do that. The two homes were just a walk away from each other.

On January 16, 1945, Emma died at the young age of 51. Virgie was 29, married with young children at the time. John & Emma's youngest child, Melvin, was just 8 years old. My grandma Esther was 16. Emma's last days were a very difficult time for everyone in the family.

The photos tucked behind her obituary at left are of Emma in her casket before burial.

Emma's last wishes

Among other things, I'm sure, there were two desires that Emma had before passing away and leaving this earthly world. First, she wanted to live long enough to see her youngest child, Melvin, be baptized. He was baptized on his 8th birthday in November, just a couple of months before Emma's death. This photo was taken of Emma and her "baby" Melvin around that time.

Also, she really wanted Grannie Marion (her mother-in-law) to come spend Christmas with them. The Marions didn't really have Christmas traditions in the sense of exchanging gifts and decorating and that sort of things, so they didn't come to visit at Christmas time. But the month before her death, Grannie Marion did go to the Jones' home where Emma was staying, and had Christmas with them. Emma died just a few weeks later.

Note from Becky: Virgie Millard (my great aunt) is my resource for this information. I spoke to her about her mother's death in April 2006 and Virgie was 90 years old at the time. I am grateful for my conversations with her … and for her memory!

MRS. EMMA V. MARION

Mount Airy.—Funeral services for Mrs. Emma V. Marion, 51, wife of John W. Marion, who died Wednesday night at the home of her mother on Taylor Street, will be held this afternoon at 2 o'clock at Sheltontown Mormon Church. David Hiatt and Elder Jimmy Hiatt will conduct the services. Burial will be in the church grave-yard.

Surviving are the husband; her mother; three sons, John Lee, Wendell and Melvin Marion, all of the home; three daughters, Mrs. Troy F. Millard, Mrs. Herman Voncannon and Miss Esther Marion, all of Mount Airy; six grandchildren; four sisters, Mrs. James Chappell, Mrs. Frank Phillips, Misses Annie and Pearlie Jones, all of Mount Airy and three brothers, Robert T. Jones of Cana, Va., and Calvin and Carva Jones of Mount Airy.

a battle lost to colon cancer

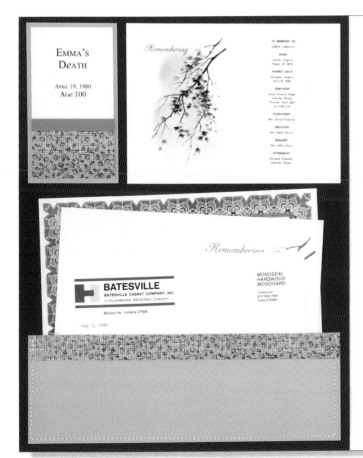

EMMA'S
DEATH

APRIL 19, 1980
AGE 100

This is to certify that this is a true and correct reproduction of the original record filed with the Arlington Department of Human Resources Arlington, Virginia.

Date Issued April 23, 1980

(seal)

ANY REPRODUCTION OF THIS DOCUMENT IS PROHIBITED BY STATUTE. DO NOT ACCEPT UNLESS IT BEARS THE IMPRESSED SEAL OF THE ARLINGTON DEPARTMENT OF HUMAN RESOURCES CLEARLY AFFIXED.

Section 32-353-27, Code of Virginia, as Amended.

Question:

I want to understand how some of my qualities and traits (hobbies, likes, dislikes, the way I look) connect with someone else in my family. How can I best discover and scrapbook my family connections?

It's amazing to discover and explore family connections. When you find out more about your family, you'll automatically discover more about yourself. My "Mothers and Daughters" layout is one of my favorite family history projects. It makes me feel happy to reflect on the people in the layout, to remember their special qualities, to celebrate our common bond of motherhood and to understand how I developed my own parenting style.

Examine photographs to find what genetic traits may be shared among your family members. Look at the physical traits. For example, my son has my eyes. My nephew has my grandpa's ears. Perhaps your daughter has your great-grandmother's hair.

You can also look for connections that involve shared interests and hobbies. Scrapbooking and family history are two of my most favorite creative outlets. I look back at my female relatives and see a strong interest in crafting—for example, my mother is a cross-stitcher and her mother was a quilter. For you scrapbookers, I bet you'll find it fascinating to go back in your family line and find relatives who had interests and talents in both crafts and photography!

"Look at my Nose," This was a term that my grandpa used. He will always be remembered as saying it. Hundreds of children passed through his studio door and heard this phrase when he tried to get each child to smile. Sometimes, I was that child. Now, as an adult, I try to use his clever trick to get my young subjects to smile. It worked much better for him.

I am not sure if my grandpa's talent wore off on me, but I know his love of photography did. He was amazing at his chosen career, and I am inspired by his life's work. I think I inherited his "eye", but I have a long way to go before I come close to his knowledge base, so I will keep working and keep studying his example.

Mothers and Daughters

Among all of the photographs I'm coming across as I work on family history, these are among my favorites. My great grandmother, my grandma, and my mom—each with their own daughters. And now that I have a daughter, I can't help but wonder how things might have been similar between all of us. I love having babies now in so different than their experiences. After all, I had an epidural for my labor & delivery, we use disposable diapers, safely strap our babies in car seats, and call a "mama" to sometimes have multiple loads of laundry in a day.

Emma Victoria Jones Marion
with her first daughter, Virgie (my grandmother's oldest sister)

in 1915

Esther Charity Marion Johnson
with her only daughter, Vicki (my mother)

in 1949

Victoria (Vicki) Elizabeth Johnson Allgaier
with her only daughter, Becky (me)

in 1977

Rebecca (Becky) Allgaier Higgins
with my daughter, Claire Esther

in 2006

But love was always around. It goes back as far as the beginning of human existence and will never go out of style. Did these mothers feel the joy that I feel when I peek in Claire's room to watch her sleeping soundly? Did they nibble on their children's necks to get a laugh, just as I do with my children? What songs did they sing to their daughters? Did they rejoice in motherhood, as I do? I love my mom and grandma so much. I would have liked to have known my great grandmothers, but do enjoy getting a little more familiar with them through doing family history.

Question:

How should I choose which photographs to scrapbook?
Do I need to scrapbook all of them?

First, I want to remind you that you don't need to scrapbook every single photograph in your possession. That could feel quite overwhelming, and I want you to enjoy scrapbooking your family history.

Second, you might have some pictures that are almost duplicates, and of course, you won't want to keep creating the same scrapbook pages over and over again. But don't just completely disregard similar photographs, either. Take a close look at them and see if you can discover details in one photograph that aren't apparent in another one. Consider storing extra photographs in an album with slip-in sleeves, like the one shown below. The checklist at right will give you a good starting point for examining your photographs for extra details.

Third, at this point in the discovery process, you'll want to make sure you have the photographs that will help tell the family stories you want to share. If you don't, ask your family members if they can help you fill in any gaps.

Checklist

As you go through your family history information, you'll discover photographs that have similarities. In fact, at first glance, these photographs might look exactly the same (and if they are, you'll probably just want to file those extra photographs). But I encourage you to take a second look. Are there any extra details that show up in one photograph that don't show up in another? This list will help you know what to look for:

1. Street signs

2. House addresses (numbers)

3. School names

4. License plate numbers

5. Bumper stickers on cars

6. Titles of books that people are holding and/or reading

7. Fashion details (Did your great-aunt always wear a pearl necklace?)

8. Facial expressions (Did you relatives smile naturally for the camera, or did they prefer to strike a pose?)

9. Tools and equipment (Is your grandmother sitting at a typewriter?)

10. Restaurant signs

*

*

*

{ **Question:**
I've discovered that my great-grandfather was an architect.
How can I learn more about the projects he worked on, and how
can I incorporate stories of his life's work into my album? }

As you discover more about a relative's career choices, I bet you'll discover more about your relative as a person. Whether your family member was an architect, a lawyer, an actress or a seamstress, you'll find all sorts of interesting documents that will help you gain important insight into that person's life. Here are a few queries that might help you in your discovery process:

＊ Did your relative work with any sort of documents? Can you find a sewing pattern from a seamstress or a house plan from an architect?

＊ Did your relative ever put together a resume? (Resumes are great for layouts because they're such a concise summary of what that person believed to be his or her top talents and skills.)

＊ Did your relative belong to any professional societies? Can you find brochures or pamphlets that relate to a membership in a professional society?

＊ Did your relative win any awards for his or her contribution to society?

＊ Why did your relative choose his or her field of work? Where did he or she go to college, or to apprentice or train for the position?

elsie
as alice
and other adventures

Elsie was born in 1908. She went to local schools in Berwyn which is near Chicago Illinois. She attended college at the Goodwin Theater Company in Chicago where she studied as an actress. In approximately 1929 a former student at the Goodwin Theater Company was working at Tony Sarge marionettes and requested that Elsie come to New York to try out for the lead in the production 'Alice in Wonderland'. Tony Sarge was famous for designing marionettes and later was acclaimed for his Macy balloon floats designs. While in New York, Elsie resided at an all girls hotel for young actresses, where she met some of her life long friends. She was selected for the lead role in the production, in which Elsie acted as Alice in a live performance and then performed the marionette part as Alice descended into the rabbit hole. She met Rhys Williams at the marionette company and within two years they were married. The marionette company toured the famous hotels in Florida, which were winter resorts for the 'snow birds' in the North East to escape the cold. The troupe traveled by train to the various locations and lived out of steamer boxes. There were many other shows that Elsie and Rhys performed manipulating marionettes. She then became part of a Shakespeare troupe that entertained at the Chicago World's fair (1933 to 1934) and later the New York World's fair (1939-1940). In between these engagements, the troupe then became the first performing company at the old Globe Theater in San Diego (1935 to 1936). During the summer months, the acting troupe often went to act in a variety of plays in summer stock in the cooler part of Maine. Many of these plays went on tour similar to today's musicals and Elsie was part of the touring. In 1941 Elsie settled in Los Angeles. In 1943 Evan was born in New York as Rhys was in a play with Helen Hays. In 1945 Tudor was born in Los Angeles where they have again made their home in Studio City Calif. Elsie lived in the house most of her life from 1944 on. In 1994 Elsie went home to be with the Lord.

adventure   a remarkable experience; take the risk; to venture.

Earl's Career in Pictures

Earl was a creative, thinking man.

His work with AAA, and later as the founder of Allgaier Shops, was a major part of his life. There are pages and pages of compiled information about his career in the "blue book" that Glen Allgaier (Earl's oldest son) did in 2004. Here are copies of some of the pictures from Earl's employment with AAA.

April 1956

A General Motors Proving Grounds official (right) demonstrates to Earl Allgaier, manager, driver education division, AAA traffic engineering and safety department, and Burton W. Marsh, executive director, AAA Foundation for Traffic Safety, the inner workings of one of the specially-constructed dummies used on the "Impact Sled" which simulates car crashes. The dummies, costing more than $2,000 apiece, are able to flex in the same manner as a human body and supply useful crash data for safety designers.

Taken in 1962

Earl & Edsel Ford at Ford Good Driver's League Contest N.Y. World's Fair in 1940.

JOURNALING LIFE ROLES

Question:

I'm discovering that my grandmother was involved in many different activities in her community and had many different life roles. How can I share this information in a way that will help tell her life story?

I believe that we all adopt "life roles" and that exploring these roles helps paint an accurate picture of who we are. Scrapbooking a person's life roles is a great way to gain insight into what that person valued and how he or she liked to spend her free time.

As you scrapbook life roles, you might want to focus on just one aspect of that person's life (for example, his or her career), or you might want to make up a list of everything your family member did in her life—in her career, in her family and as a hobby. For example, your great-grandmother may have been a mother, wife, friend, daughter, seamstress, quilter, healer and more.

Scrapbooking life roles also helps us broaden our perspective on a person and helps us understand that person's personality traits. For example, a friend's great-grandfather was known as "a farmer," but he was also hard-working, reliable, intensely loyal to his wife and family, ambitious and driven. Learning these "extra" things about her ancestor helped her gain a new respect for him and what he passed down to other people in their family line.

I wish to **Live Deliberately**

...live deep and suck out all the marrow of life... and not when I had come to die discover that I had not lived."

(The Incomplete List of my Parent's Life Roles)

Dad: Sertoma· Chamber of Commerce· Town and Country Days· Economic Development· New Life 200 St. Teresa· State MPHA Board of Directors and other Pharmaceutical organizations· Pharmacist· Father· Community Member· Brother· Friend· Cutler· Business Owner· Son· Dreamer· Gardener· Boss· Band Member· Barbershops·

Mom: Girl Scouts· CCD Instructor· Cub Scouts· PACE· School Volunteer· Town and Country Days· CCW President· Day Care Provider· New Life 2000· St. Teresa· Poll Volunteer· Church Finance Council· Mother· Business Owner· Community Member· Sister· Daughter· Shopper· Gardener·Friend· Boss· Organizer·

active be

His Work

The man was talented. No doubt about that. These are some scans and photographs of some of Earl's original drawings, mostly from the late 1930's and 1940's.

Earl Allgaier

Question:
How do I scrapbook my family history when I have so many unanswered questions?

Believe me, I've talked with many scrapbookers who get frustrated at this point in the process. I understand that it can feel difficult to create pages when you just don't have all the answers you'd like. As I suggested earlier, keep a list of unanswered questions and do as much research as you can to find at least a few answers. If you can't find the answers, it's just fine to create pages centered around your unanswered questions. Consider these options:

✱ Make a layout where the journaling *is* the unanswered questions.

✱ Create an album that's just about your unanswered questions. Include unidentified photographs along with your questions. Take this album with you to every single family gathering you attend. You just might run into a relative who can give you crucial information that will turn your questions into answers!

✱ Fill in the gaps with what you imagine might be true and research on the Internet to add historical information to your page.

✱ Make a note of where you found your photographs and documents, and acknowledge that you don't have all of the answers. An example? "These photographs were found in my great-aunt Lora's attic at the time of her death. I don't know who many of the people in these pictures are, but I do know that these photographs must have been important to her."

Checklist

When you have unanswered questions about your family history, you may feel as though you're lost in the middle of a giant maze! Trying to find all of the answers will take time and patience. And, you may not be able to find all the answers. You can, however, use your questions as journaling jumpstarts. Use the following prompts to help start the process on your next layout (plus, they can also be used for interviewing family members):

1. I wonder how my grandparents met each other and what their courtship was like.

2. I wonder how my great-grandmother felt when her sons went to war.

3. I wonder what it was like for my grandparents to grow up during the Depression.

4. I wonder why my grandfather chose his profession, or I wonder how the family business got started.

5. I have a family recipe that's been passed down through generations. I wonder what the story is behind it.

6. We have three generations of men who like to fish in my family. Where did this hobby get its start?

7. I wonder what my mother was like as a child. What were her favorite toys, games and classes in school?

8. Many generations of my family have followed one religion. I wonder which member of my family converted first and what his or her conversion story is.

9. I wonder why my parents gave me the name they did. What other names were they considering? I wonder if I was planned. I wonder if they already knew the gender.

10. My family has lived in California for generations. I wonder which family member came here first and why.

*

I made this scrapbook to honor my father—a man who spent his life in the service of others. I feel it's important that my children and future generations come know the many contributions he made to his family, his church and his country. Here's the five-step process I followed to complete it:

1. GATHER. I collected photographs and stories about my father.

2. SORT. As I looked through my photographs, I thought about how my father had spent his life contributing to others. I started to sort my photographs into categories, such as family and church.

3. PREPARE/ORGANIZE. I made a list of the specific categories I wanted to include in this album.

4. DISCOVER. I did some basic research and discovered the information I needed to tell the stories I wanted to share.

5. PRESENT. I followed a simple format for this album to keep the focus on the story and the photographs.

—Tori Howell

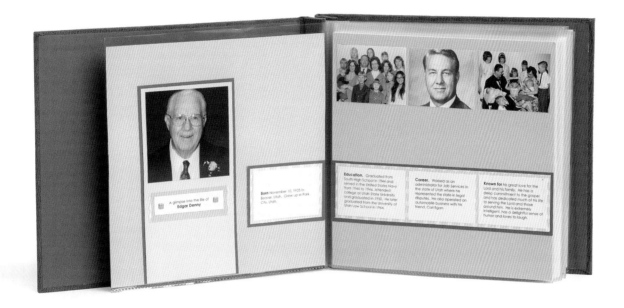

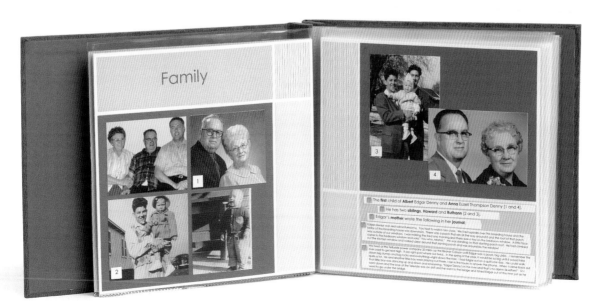

*W*ouldn't it be great to see pictures of your ancestors of the same gender in one place? Because I'm female, I chose to highlight several generations of directly related female ancestors in an eye-catching photographic

To begin, I gathered photos of my mom, grandmas, great-grandmothers and so forth. Then I choose a frame with multiple spaces for photos. (You can find them at stores like Target, Wal-Mart and Costco; I actually found this one at Bombay Kids.) I printed my pictures to fit in the frames and, before slipping them inside, tied several short pieces of various ribbons between all of the pictures. It's a fun and easy way to add a feminine touch and a great way to use all that ribbon you're hoarding ... I mean collecting.

Use this worksheet to help you prepare and organize your family history.

1. What questions do you have about your family history at this point in the process? Which questions would you like to answer first?

_____

_____

_____

2. What resources can you utilize as you seek to discover more about your family history?

_____

_____

_____

3. At this point in your family history project, what topics feel most inspirational to you?

_____

_____

_____

4. How can you enlist other family members to help you discover more about your family history?

_____

_____

5. What discoveries have you already made that feel exciting and interesting to you? How can you continue to pursue these topics?

_____

_____

_____

_____

6. What are you discovering about yourself as you work through this process?

_____

_____

_____

SCHOOL for Carl

Carl and his siblings attended the Artesia
school. Their education took place in a one-room
school in the town of Artesia just a couple of
miles away from the Higgins homestead. Artesia,
located at the foot of Mount Graham, was a small
farming community about ten miles from Safford
with natural hot artesian springs.

Carl attended through the 8th grade and this may
have been the only school he ever attended. Of
the 15 Higgins kids, just three of the nine
sisters are shown in this picture. One was
married and 5 were too young for school. Two of
Carl's brothers are in the picture since two
were already working and one was too young.

For a moment, I'd like you to use your imagination. Imagine you had an ancestor who was like you and wanted to get all of her family history in order. She gathered everything in one place, sorted through all of the photos and memorabilia, got totally organized and was ready to scrapbook. Wow, impressive, right?

Now imagine you have the chance to give this person some advice on how to present it all. This is your chance to tell her what you hope to receive one day. What would you want her to do? Really think about this. Do you want her to include only a few photos and minimal information because she spent all of her time being "artistic"?

Me? I want to see more photos. I want to read more journaling. Tell me interesting facts, share experiences and stories. I want detail. I want to have a very real sense of what my progenitors were like, how they lived, what they loved.

In other words, I would want my ancestor to spend her time preserving the photos and stories more than trying to create a masterpiece with each scrapbook page.

As you create the scrapbook pages that celebrate your family heritage, keep the focus on the photographs and the stories. Keeping your albums classic, simple and richly informative will leave you with no regrets. Here, I'll show you how.

Question:

Becky, what's your philosophy for
scrapbooking your family history pages?

We all like making beautiful pages, but I believe that family history scrapbooking is not about me or my creativity. Out of respect for my ancestors, I think it's important to keep my pages simple. I want the focus to be on the photographs and the stories, and not so much on which embellishments I selected or what techniques I decided to try.

I let go of the pressure to be creative on my family history pages, knowing that I can be creative on my current scrapbooking projects. You'll see throughout this book that my layouts all have a similar look—classic and simple. They have a cardstock background, photographs, documents and some journaling. These layouts may not be "fancy," but they do have an appeal that might get lost on an overly done page.

Question:

How should I start my album?

I think every album should have an introduction, which may include any of the following items: a forward (perhaps a short discussion of the album's purpose or a letter explaining why you decided to create the album), a dedication page (where you dedicate the album to a certain person or couple in your family line), and/or a table of contents (where you clearly state which pages the reader will find in the album). An opening page, even if it's just a simple statement of why you created the album, will help your readers understand the scope of the album. You might also want to consider opening your album with a family tree or a list of the names of the people (and their relationships to each other) who you celebrate in the album.

If you're working on an entire set of albums, it might be helpful to label your album by family name, by decade and/or by topic. If you know the album is the third in a series of 10, you might want to include that information in your introduction as well. This way, future generations won't wonder how many albums there are altogether and will know if a certain album is missing from the series.

Question:

*I want my family history pages to be beautiful, but
I feel overwhelmed when I start thinking about the amount
of time I'll need to complete each layout. Any advice?*

As scrapbookers, we all want to create beautiful pages. After all, we're creating albums we want our future generations to cherish and enjoy. But if we don't have time to make these pages, then they'll never be enjoyed. Don't worry about making each page an artistic masterpiece—your family will love your pages no matter how you tell your stories.

My best advice is to let go of the pressure to be exceptionally creative on your family history pages. I absolutely love the layouts in this book; if you take a close look at them, you'll notice that the designers employed techniques that made their pages simple, appealing and uniquely their own.

Also, I think family history is a great place to be creative in terms of how you present information (for example, through a timeline or a bulleted list) or in terms of how you tell a story (through the words and illustrations you choose to share a family legend, for instance).

Take a look at the checklist here, which shares some of my favorite ideas for creating scrapbook pages that are simply beautiful.

Checklist

Need ideas on how to keep your pages simple yet beautiful? Here's a list of my favorite techniques that will help you keep the focus on your photographs and stories:

1. Choose a basic black, white or tan background.

2. Choose a basic template for each album and stick to it.

3. Set aside a couple of hours to handwrite or computer-generate your journaling for your pages.

4. Sketch outlines of your layouts beforehand.

5. Use excerpts of letters or newspaper clippings for the journaling instead of writing it yourself.

6. Limit yourself to five products total for an entire layout.

7. Consider choosing just one or two fonts for a particular family history project.

8. Create white space. It makes a layout less cluttered and easier to read.

9. Remember that you don't need to scrapbook all your photos. Choose just a few that really capture personality and character and use only those. File the rest away.

10. Scraplifting is not a crime! Use this book to get great ideas instead of trying to come up with every design on your own.

Question:

*I want to share my family history project
with other people in my family.
How can I best accomplish this goal?*

The Internet is a wonderful tool for family historians. As I've shared before, I love using the Internet to do research. I also love that I can share photographs and scrapbook pages on the Internet with my family members; we even have a website just for that purpose. I must say, it's a huge relief and a great way to save time. No need to create an album for everyone in your family! Instead, post the information on the Internet. You'll be surprised by how much this will reduce your stress.

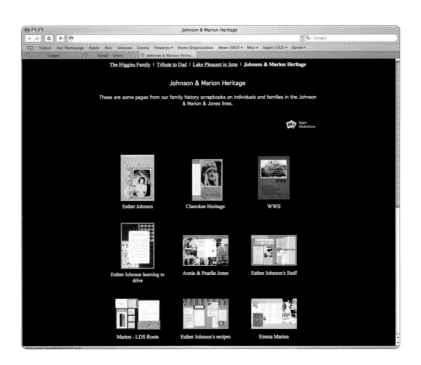

Checklist

ONLINE SHARING

With today's technology, it's easy to share your family history information electronically. It's a real bonus to be able to share (virtually for free and with no mailing costs!) photographs and information with family members who live around the world. Try these ideas for sharing your family history information with your family members:

1. Set up a family blog through a site like *www.blogspot.com* (free) or *www.typepad.com* (minimal monthly fee).

2. Have a techno-savvy family member set up a family website where you can share stories, announcements, photographs and completed family history pages. A web cam can be fun, too.

3. Share photographs through online photo processing/sharing sites such as *www.snapfish.com.*

4. Set up a family message board through a genealogy website, such as *www.ancestry.com.*

5. Communicate with people who share your surname at *www.genforum.com.*

6. Use a networking site, such as *www.friendster.com,* to share information about each member of your family. I have a friend who enjoys keeping up with her brother this way.

{ **Question:**
*How can I share several years' worth
of information in an easy but
visually appealing way?* }

Scrapbooking in a timeline format is an easy way to share quite a bit of information at once. On Carey's timeline at right, you'll see how she included school colors and bulleted highlights from every year of college. My timeline, of Earl and Esther's church service, includes color-coded information that shows who did what.

You can use a timeline for almost anything on a layout. How about a timeline of education (from kindergarten to college), child-rearing (from the birth of a new baby to the last child's graduation) or a relationship (from the first date to the first wedding anniversary)?

Maroon and Gold

GOLDEN GOPHERS · GOLDEN GOPHERS · GOLDEN GOPHERS · GOLDEN GOPHERS

The Years
College

1964-1965
*Spat Camp (band)
*Dorms
*Engineering
*Played in Iowa
*Studied A LOT

Band

1965-1966
*Played at the Vice President Inauguration in D.C
*Lived in a house
*Trumpet

1966-1967
*Change to Pharmacy major
*Joined Kappa Si
*Played at Perdue
*Crooked roommate

University M Minnesota

Love

Goals

1967-1968
*Love Pharmacy school
*Switched to Mello phone.
*1st Bridge tourney

1968-1969
*Met Mary
*Got engaged
*Earned band blanket
*Graduated

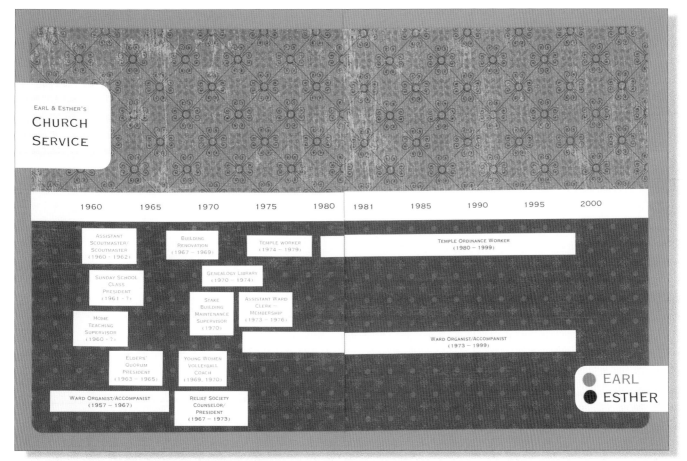

EARL & ESTHER'S
CHURCH SERVICE

| 1960 | 1965 | 1970 | 1975 | 1980 | 1981 | 1985 | 1990 | 1995 | 2000 |

ASSISTANT SCOUTMASTER/ SCOUTMASTER (1960 - 1962)

BUILDING RENOVATION (1967 - 1969)

TEMPLE WORKER (1974 - 1979)

TEMPLE ORDINANCE WORKER (1980 - 1999)

SUNDAY SCHOOL CLASS PRESIDENT (1961 - ?)

GENEALOGY LIBRARY (1970 - 1974)

HOME TEACHING SUPERVISOR (1960 - ?)

STAKE BUILDING MAINTENANCE SUPERVISOR (1970)

ASSISTANT WARD CLERK — MEMBERSHIP (1973 - 1976)

WARD ORGANIST/ACCOMPANIST (1973 - 1999)

ELDERS' QUORUM PRESIDENT (1963 - 1965)

YOUNG WOMEN VOLLEYBALL COACH (1969, 1970)

WARD ORGANIST/ACCOMPANIST (1957 - 1967)

RELIEF SOCIETY COUNSELOR/ PRESIDENT (1967 - 1973)

EARL
ESTHER

CREATING SIMPLE PAGES

Question:
*I want to keep my pages visually simple.
How can I make them look appealing?*

One of my favorite techniques for creating a visually simple background is to start with either white or black cardstock. Don't be afraid of plain white cardstock! It can actually be quite beautiful, and if you want to dress it up a bit, consider buying a higher-quality white cardstock. Most old black-and-white photographs will probably have some discoloration or spots, and when you place them on a basic white background, you'll have a better view of the original photograph. It will look true-to-life and have an authentic feel.

Your photographs and journaling will also shine on a black background. There won't be anything to distract you. And black backgrounds were once quite popular in old-time scrapbooks—they'll add classic appeal to your pages.

The
EARLY
DAYS
of the farm

These pictures are the first known to be taken in the farmhouse soon after they moved in. For the most part, it looked much different than I (Becky, their granddaughter) remember it to be. My memories of the house include a lot more "stuff". So these were taken before I had many memories at all. The two pictures on this page are the main living area (downstairs) and the bathroom, which was upstairs by the bedrooms. On the facing page (top left), that is just inside the back door, which was really the only door used. The top right picture is their dining room, and then the kitchen at bottom left (I'm not certain who the woman sitting with Esther is ... a friend, I'm sure). The bottom right picture is the bedroom at the front of the house. All of the bedrooms were upstairs. I do not remember it looking like this at all, but apparently they decorated it like this for the granddaughters (mainly me since I lived locally and visited more often). My memory of that room is that my grandma used it for sewing and it was loaded with fabric. I enjoyed playing in there. Another bedroom was painted purple (my mother's favorite color).

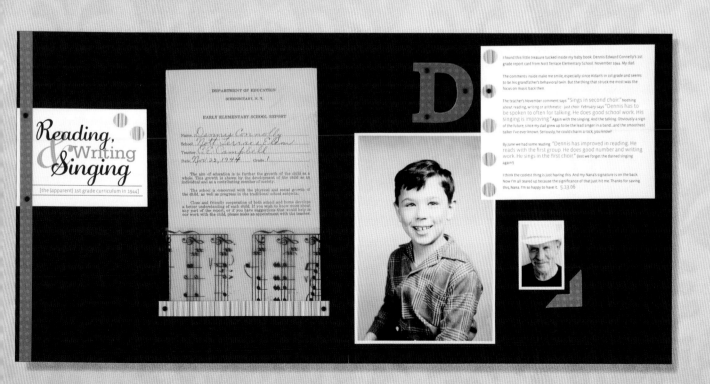

Reading, & Writing Singing

[the (apparent) 1st grade curriculum in 1944]

DEPARTMENT OF EDUCATION
SCHENECTADY, N.Y.

EARLY ELEMENTARY SCHOOL REPORT

Name: Dennis Connolly
School: Nott Terrace Elem
Teacher: C.E. Campbell
Date: Nov. 22, 1944   Grade: 1

The aim of education is to further the growth of the child as a whole. This growth is shown by the development of the child as an individual and as a contributing member of society.

The school is concerned with the physical and social growth of the child, as well as progress in the traditional school subjects.

Close and friendly cooperation of both school and home develops a better understanding of each child. If you wish to know more about any part of the report, or if you have suggestions that would help in our work with the child, please make an appointment with the teacher.

I found this little treasure tucked inside my baby book. Dennis Edward Connelly's 1st grade report card from Nott Terrace Elementary School, November 1944. My dad.

The comments inside make me smile, especially since Aidan's in 1st grade and seems to be his grandfather's behavioral twin. But the thing that struck me most was the focus on music back then.

The teacher's November comment says "Sings in second choir." Nothing about reading, writing or arithmetic - just choir. February says "Dennis has to be spoken to often for talking. He does good school work. His singing is improving." Again with the singing. And the talking. Obviously a sign of the future, since my dad grew up to be the lead singer in a band...and the smoothest talker I've ever known. Seriously, he could charm a rock, you know?

By June we had some reading "Dennis has improved in reading. He reads with the first group. He does good number and writing work. He sings in the first choir." (lest we forget the darned singing again)

I think the coolest thing is just having this. And my Nana's signature is on the back. Now I'm all teared up because the significance of that just hit me. Thanks for saving this, Nana. I'm so happy to have it.   5.13.06

SELECTING PATTERNED PAPERS

{
Question:
*I want to add patterned paper
to my family history layouts.
Can you share some tips with me?*
}

There are several companies that offer patterned papers with a classic and timeless appeal that's perfect for heritage pages. You'll see a sampling of these papers throughout this book. When choosing patterned paper, ask yourself the following questions—and remember, when it comes to using patterned paper on heritage layouts, less is more!

✳ Does the paper help tell the story or does it distract from the story in any way?

✳ Does the feeling or mood of the paper lend historical accuracy to your layout?

✳ Does the paper contribute to the tone of your page (happy, sad, somber, beautiful and so on)?

✳ Can you use just a small amount of patterned paper to draw attention to a key feature in a photograph? How about using it for a page border?

Becky Allgaier (me) with the unfinished product. I think I was about 8 or 9 years old and this was taken in Troy & Virgie's home.

Troy Willard. "Uncle Troy" to us. Based on our numerous family trips to North Carolina, my impression of him is that he was a quiet man. I don't remember him talking very much and it seems that he often sat in "his" chair in the front room that had the TV. Troy's life work was carpentry. Virgie says he really enjoyed being a carpenter. He also worked in a furniture factory for a couple of years but he really didn't like being inside all the time, so he went back to carpentry. He never ran a formal business. He worked for different companies and sometimes for himself. After retiring, he continued doing little projects – furniture and crafts. Troy loved working with his hands and he was very talented. I benefited from his skills as a young girl. He made me this set – a baby dresser and high chair. My parents recently came across the dresser (the mirror is missing or possibly it broke & was thrown away years ago?) and we do not know where the high chair is. I remember loving these and since I had so many dolls and stuffed animals, the baby furniture definitely came in handy.

Recent photos of little dresser (shown above) taken in 2006.

Side note: My mother, Vicki Allgaier, said that Troy was a good man who had a problem with drinking and therefore had a difficult time holding down any job for very long. A lot of these were "odd jobs". Virgie (Troy's wife) confirmed that he did indeed have various jobs over the years but I didn't ask her about the drinking. As a young girl, I knew he was a heavy smoker.

Question:

*How do I find time to work on
my family history projects?*

This is a fantastic question. We're all busy with our lives, our families and our current scrapbook projects! It can feel almost impossible to add another project to the list. But, there are ways to fit this sort of project into your schedule. Try these options:

✻ Be willing to work in stages. I'm usually working on several albums at the same time. It's perfectly okay to have unfinished albums that are in-process.

✻ Set aside time to scrapbook each week. Can you dedicate 30 minutes? How about an hour? Schedule time to work on these projects.

✻ Follow the steps in this book or create your own family history plan. You'll be much happier and less overwhelmed if you have a system you can use to make scrapbooking less stressful.

✻ Set a realistic goal for yourself. Tell yourself that you want to create one family history layout each week (or more if you feel you can!). I bet you'll be able to do it once you get started.

✻ Make it easy for yourself. Remember, you don't have to scrapbook every picture; it's perfectly fine to store extra photographs and documents in sheet protectors.

✻ Keep your eye on the prize. Family history scrapbooking is really special. Make it fun for yourself and think about how much the completed albums will be treasured and enjoyed!

jake & esther johnson's farm

[yarrowsburg, maryland]

the farm
a series of pages about jake & esther's farm

the STORY

Jake & Esther lived in Silver Spring, MD, just outside of Washington, D.C. They often would drive out in the country and one day they came across a "for sale" sign in Yarrowsburg, a rural community in Washington County (just barely outside of Frederick County). This 5-acre farmette was very appealing to them and they decided to buy it and move their life to the country. Jake moved his business to the nearby town of Brunswick. Wayne & Vicki (their daughter) ended up moving to Brunswick the following year (1974) when Wayne completed his service in Guam. Located only 5-10 miles from the farm, they would visit often. Jake & Esther loved it in Yarrowsburg. Their next-door neighbors, Bill & Doris, became good friends. Jake had a love for tractors and that sort of thing and I imagine they both enjoyed a slower pace of life. Unfortunately, their marriage ended and Jake moved his life and his work back to Silver Spring. Things at the farm started to go downhill as Esther was not able to maintain the home and property on her own. Jake bought her a home in Mt. Airy, NC, across the street from her oldest sister Virgie. He kept the farm and when he died, it was part of his estate, which went to Jake and Esther's children.

The farm address was a P.O Box in Knoxville, MD 21758

---

picnics at the farm

the farm
a series of pages about jake & esther's farm

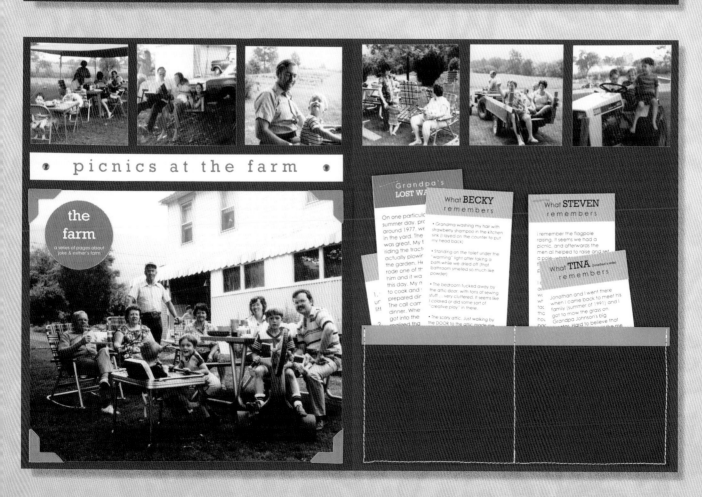

Grandpa's LOST WA...

On one particul... summer day, pro... around 1977, we... in the yard. The... was great. My f... riding the tract... actually plowi... the garden. He... rode one of t... him and it wa... this day. My n... to cook and... prepared di... The call cam... dinner. Whe... got into the... ...mized tha...

What **BECKY** remembers

• Grandma washing my hair with strawberry shampoo in the kitchen sink (I layed on the counter to put my head back)

• Standing on the toilet under the "warming" light after taking a bath while we dried off (that bathroom smelled so much like powder)

• The bedroom tucked away by the attic door, with tons of sewing stuff ... very cluttered. It seems like I colored or did some sort of "creative play" in there.

• The scary attic. Just walking by the DOOR to the attic made me...

What **STEVEN** remembers

I remember the flagpole raising. It seems we had a picnic, and afterwards the men all helped to raise and set a pole...

What **TINA** (Jonathan's wife) remembers

Jonathan and I went there when I came back to meet his family (summer of 1991) and I got to mow the grass on Grandpa Johnson's big... ...tor. Hard to believe that...

CREATING A UNIFIED ALBUM

Question:

What's the best way to create flow and
continuity in my albums? I want them to all work
together and feel like they are parts of the whole.

The best way to create flow in your albums is to start with a
basic plan before you create your first page. Here's how:

✳ Start with a sketch (or two) that you can repeat throughout your
   project. All you really need is one or two sketches that you love
   and that will provide appropriate places for your photographs,
   documents and journaling.

✳ Decide on a journaling style for your pages and stick with it throughout each album. For example, will you handwrite or computer-
   generate your journaling? Will you write your stories in first person
   or third person? (More on this a bit later in this chapter.)

✳ Choose a basic color scheme. Keep it simple by choosing a basic black
   or white background for all of your pages, or branch out a bit by
   choosing muted pastels with a bit of patterned paper for emphasis.

✳ Be consistent in your page design, and you'll find they'll automatically
   come together in an album that feels unified, even if you work out
   of order or work on your pages in stages. Both of the title pages at
   right are the beginning of these ancestors' respective sections in our
   family history albums. I kept the overall design the same, which is
   carried through each of the sections.

Marjorie Esther Brand Stewart

Orson & Tillie Foote

Question:

How do I summarize a lengthy family history into just one album?

This sounds like a huge challenge, doesn't it? I want to assure you that it can be done and that it's a great approach to take with your family history. Review your mission statement (decide what you want to accomplish with your album) and then consider these possible approaches:

✳ I helped a friend of mine create an album that has one layout for each individual in her family. The layouts all have the same simple format. Each person's layout has a place for information about that person, as well as little pocket sleeves where she can tuck additional stories and anecdotes. As you can see on pg 129, these pages can easily be replicated.

✳ See Joanna Bolick's pages at the bottom of page 129? She created a family history album that focuses on couples in her family history. Each couple has a page that includes a photograph from their wedding and information about their jobs, kids and general lives.

✳ Create an album that focuses on your ancestors' lives through the decades, such as a summary of your family in 1910, 1920, 1930 and so on. Include relevant photographs and facts on each page.

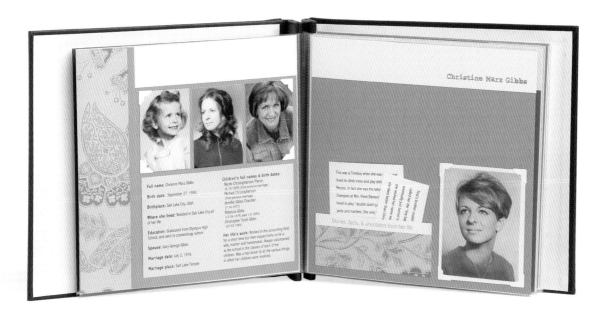

JOURNALING VOICES

Question:
*When I write my journaling,
what "voice" should I use?*

In most cases, I think it's best to write in a third-person voice, for example: "Mary was born in 1945 and grew up in Brooklyn, New York, with her parents and her three sisters."

Occasionally, you may want to write in the first-person voice, but make sure to clarify that you're not quoting the individual. For example, on my "Johan" layout, my dad wrote the journaling as if Johan is talking to the reader, but in small print, I clarified that it was my dad who wrote the journaling, not Johan.

If you have notes or journaling written in your family member's voice, it's wonderful to include their words as they were written. Make sure to include a bit of information on your page to let your reader know the source of the information, such as, "I discovered these words, in Mary's own handwriting, in the journal she kept from 1964–1973."

Whatever voice you choose, it's a good idea to keep it consistent throughout your album.

My name is **Johan Martin Allgaier.**

I was the third of four children born to Johan Michael Allgaier, born 11 August 1821, at a time when things seemed to be settling down politically in Germany and our kingdom of Bavaria. Our king was Ludwig I, who reigned from 1825 to 1848, when he abdicated to Maximillian II during the German Revolution. The end of Ludwig's reign came at a difficult time, not only politically, but also economically. A four-year famine had made things very difficult, and unemployment was a major problem.

With all of this going on, and reports of unlimited land and employment coming from America, I began to think seriously about going there. It would be difficult to leave my family and my native land, but there was no promise of a future here.

So I finally made the decision to follow many of my fellow countrymen and immigrated to America in 1852 (at the age of 31), going to the city of Chicago.

I married Verena Brunner, and our first child Emil was born in Chicago on 12 June 1855. Six months later we bought property in Kankakee (40 miles south of Chicago), where our other two children were born - Adolf (31 Jan 1857) and Bertha (February 1859).

Johan died in the early 1860's not quite 40 years old, leaving his wife to raise their three young children.

This was really written by Wayne Allgaier, Johan's great-great grandson, who compiled the information.

Milagros Jalgalado Cavida, know by friends and family as Mely, graduated from Philippine Union College in Cavite with a Bachelors of Science in Nursing in 1963. Mely was the youngest child of Laureano and Maria Cavida of Lucban, Quezon, simple farmers in a small town at the foot of Mt. Banahaw on the island of Luzon. Among her nine siblings, Mely was the second to earn a college degree and the first to become a professional in the medical field. Her older brother Eben, the youngest of the three boys in the family, had earned a degree in accounting and helped pay for her college education.

Not long after becoming a nurse, opportunity arose that enabled Mely to work as a nurse in the United States. She, along with two of her friends who had graduated with her from nursing school, Flor Penaflorida and Virginia Vingco, left their lives and their families behind to work as nurses in Chicago, Illinois. The three young nurses who were the first of their families to go to the United States, looked forward to life in America. However, they sorely missed their families and their homeland. After a few years of working in the States, Mely decided to go back home to the Philippines, and she worked at Manila Sanitarium and Hospital.

Mely spent just a few years back home in the Philippines. She returned to the United States at the urging of her father. He convinced her that many more opportunities for a better life were available for her in the U.S. She went back to the Chicago area and worked at Hinsdale Sanitarium and Hospital in the western

suburbs. With time Mely became an American citizen and married Bonifacio "Boni" Fernandez, an auto mechanic, who was also from the Philippines and the first from his family to immigrate to America. The two of them lived in Chicago where Mely continued to work as a nurse at Roosevelt Hospital. Mely and Boni had two daughters, Melanie Joy and Marife Aimee. When the girls were toddlers, Mely supported the family while Boni went to school for a two-year degree in Respiratory Therapy at Northwestern University.

Before their girls were of school age, Mely and Boni decided to move their family to the western suburbs. Mely went back to work at Hinsdale Hospital as a post-partum care nurse in the maternity unit. She worked in post-partum care for more than twenty years until she retired from nursing in December 2003, one month after her first grandchild, Cadence Joy Uzarraga, was born. The following year, Mely's two grandsons, Ronald Clark Uzarraga and Jacob Fernandez Capina, were born. All three of her grandchild were born at the hospital at which she dedicated half her nursing career. Mely was able to give each of her grandchildren their very first baths in the post-partum care nursery.

Since graduating in 1963, Mely worked full-time as a nurse for forty years until the day that she retired. Her journey as a nurse has certainly been a long one, but it was one filled kindness, caring and dedication. Mely cannot be replaced, but her legacy as a nurse will forever live on in the lives of those patients and their families whom she has touched.

Shortly after my grandmother died, I created this album so my daughter, who's named after my grandmother, would understand the history behind her name. I wanted her to understand that she not only inherited a name, but also a legacy. Here's a summary of the process I used to complete the album:

1. GATHER. After my grandmother's death, my mother and I went through boxes and boxes and looked for any information we could find about my grandmother. We searched for photographs, documents and letters that would give us important insights into my grandmother's life.

2. SORT. As we went through boxes of information, we pulled out information we thought would be most helpful for this project.

3. PREPARE/ORGANIZE. I made scans of all the items we gathered and started selecting what to include in the album.

4. DISCOVER. To get a better feel for who my grandmother was as a person, I read old letters from her and asked my parents to write down their memories of her.

5. PRESENT. I divided the album into two sections that explain the heritage behind her first name (named after my grandmother) and her middle name (named after me). At one point, I might decide to add a third section that explores our last name. Because my grandmother's favorite color was pink, I chose a pink color scheme (and I used a floral patterned paper because my grandmother loved flowers). At the end of the album, I included a CD that has extra information, including pedigree charts and other items.

—Laurie Scholzen

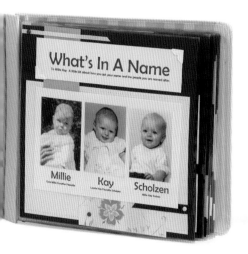

Your family history projects can be anything you'd like them to be, including something as simple as a brag book for a family member. I created this brag book for my dad because he's often asked about his family by folks at work and in the community. Now he has a little album he can pull out and share with everyone! I designed this so the photographs can easily be slipped out and replaced with current photographs as our family continues to grow and change.

A brag book is a simple and fun project you can create in a weekend. And, it's something current family members can enjoy now, and future family members can enjoy 50 years from now! To create your own brag book, start with a simple mini album. Add photographs and names or minimal journaling and you're done!

Use this worksheet to help you decide how to present your family history on scrapbook pages or in albums.

1. How will you present your family history (in a series of albums, in one album, in mini books, in a home-decor project)?

_____

_____

2. What are the top three things you want to keep in mind as you scrapbook your family history?

_____

_____

3. What design scheme will you choose for your layouts?

_____

_____

4. What sort of journaling style will you use on your layouts?

_____

_____

5. What color scheme seems most appropriate for your project?

_____

_____

6. What family history layouts in this book are most inspirational to you? What do you like best about how they present information to the reader?

_____

_____

_____

_____

Who was he?

w a r r e n   f o o t e

Born August 10, 1817

Died July 23, 1903

Eleventh of twelve children born to David and Irene Lane Foote, Warren was a farmer, bee keeper, stage driver, school teacher, miller, Post Master, Justice of the Peace, Major in the Mormon Militia, father to eleven children, and a true pioneer.

D o you feel like you're getting a grasp on all of this? Are you ready to dive into your family history full swing, or are you thinking baby steps, baby steps, baby steps? Whatever feels most doable or comfortable for you, just keep in mind that family history is a work-in-progress. Ultimately we'd like to have everything completely organized and preserved, but if you have a lot of stuff, this process will take some time.

In this last chapter, I'll address some of the other questions you may have that we haven't yet covered, like odd-sized photos, handwriting samples, missing information, missing photos, gift albums and more.

Just some parting thoughts before you finish this book: Keep it simple. (Have I mentioned that once or twice, or 12 times?) Seriously—you're potentially going to be investing a lot of time in this project. I really don't want you to feel any pressure to be "creative" with your family history.

Schedule time to work on this a little here,
a little there. Enjoy the journey.

Appreciate the lessons learned. Get your family involved. Grow closer to them as you discover new things and share your discoveries. And grow closer to your ancestors. It's my hope that you will connect with them like never before and that your experience will enrich your life and your soul.

DESIGNING WITH ODD-SIZED PHOTOS

Question:

Many of my family history photographs are odd sizes (not the standard 4" x 6" photos I have in my personal collection today). What design tips can you suggest for scrapbooking these photographs?

It can be a challenge to scrapbook odd-sized photographs, especially if you have a number of them. One solution is to scan them and resize them, but keep in mind that you might lose some detail and resolution if you play around with the pixels too much. You can also do what Lisa Brown Caveney did on her layout at right and arrange them in an attractively grouped manner.

Another tip? Look at your photographs as a series of rectangles and squares. Instead of thinking your photographs are all different sizes, consider them to be just two different shapes. Rectangular and square-shaped photographs are easier to work with in a design sense, and if you'll look at my sketches on pages 158-165, you'll see an assortment of page ideas you can easily modify to work with your existing photographs.

BROTHERS

JOHNNY AND JACOB JOHNSON

As young boys, this shows Johnny on the left and Jake on the right. The picture of the two of them as young adults in the Navy is a "famous" one in our family. While Johnny was stationed in Guam, Jake's unit stopped at the island for refueling. While there, he enquired if the 94th Battalion was on the island. Discovering that it was, he went to headquarters and was able to locate Johnny. They spent a couple of hours together, and a photographer who heard of their "reunion" took this picture of the two of them together.

CATS & DOGS

Johnny (a year or so older) and Jake were so much alike. They both thought they were right about things so, as you can imagine, they fought all the time. At the same time, they were close. They grew up very close to one another, piggybacking their way into the Navy and then moving to Maryland from North Carolina. Vicki (Jake's daughter) remembers always being at Johnny & Eva's house in Tacoma Park (which was not far from their home in Silver Spring), so obviously they spent a lot of time together, even after they were both married. This picture was taken not too long before Jake's death (and subsequently, Johnny's death).

school *photos*

SEVENTH *grade*

EIGHTH *grade*

NINTH *grade*

TENTH *grade*

ELEVENTH *grade*

TWELFTH *grade*

{ **Question:**
Any last tips that will help make my
family history projects successful? }

Enjoy the process of gathering your photographs and scrapbooking them! It's easy to get overwhelmed by the sheer volume of information you may have. Cherish your role as your family's historian, and just think—you're the one who gets to tell the family stories. You're the one who gets to write those stories down and preserve those precious photographs.

See if you can find a couple of friends who are working on family history projects. You can all share stories, tips, solutions, anecdotes and more. And, once in a while, work on a project where you're creating family history today. Document the correspondence between your mom and your son, or record a story that involves both you and your daughter.

correspondence

their long distance

Living 1,039 miles ... separated from his Nana is hard. Sure, we visit twice a year and she comes down here at least once. And they talk several times a week on the phone. But it's just not enough.

So sometime last year, Nana suggested that she and Aidan write letters to each other. I think it was sparked by the fact he needed some handwriting work, and the letters definitely increase in number just before a visit ... But no matter the reason, or the frequency, these letters are something I know they'll both treasure.

And now they have a home. I've saved Nana's letters and they're in that envelope over on the right. And Nana's saved Aidan's and they're going into the envelope on the left.

Because everything that's worth saving deserves a home. Don't you think?

a   n

a brief "overview" interview with
Ruby Mae Oleson Richards
By Sarah Jane Stohl Blamires (granddaughter)

spring 2000 • age 87

Q: Tell me what you were like as a baby.

A: Those who were waiting for me rejoiced at my coming. They loved me dearly and I returned their love by being a happy baby. They called me "Smiles." I have heard them say I never cried. Big brother, LaMar, adored me and must have been very tender and kind to me.

Q: What were you like as a child?

A: I was the second child, oldest daughter of seven, and sensed early in life my mother's need for help with the other children. I seemed to fall into this role easily, loving to help my younger siblings get ready for church, for school, telling a little brother as I was combing his hair for the first day of school, "Be sure to smile at the teacher so she'll like you."

I was a shy, quiet little girl, but had many friends in my quiet way. I think my brothers and sisters were my best friends, however. We had wonderful times growing up, learning how to work, to be responsible, and to be faithful in church attendance in our early years. My favorite birthday present was a little sister. She was born at home, twenty minutes after twelve the night of my eleventh birthday. Immediately after her arrival my father came into my bedroom, picked me up in his arms and said, "I want you to see what we got you for your birthday."

Q: Sometimes it is hard to choose the "very best day of your life", so tell me one of the best days or moments of your life.

A: The day I married my "honey". When Steve found me he wanted to get married as soon as he knew I was the one he had been looking for. He was five years older than I, and ready to settle down. One big problem- we had to wait until my brother was released from his mission. We waited. He arrived home the morning of our wedding in the Salt Lake Temple, March 29, 1940.

Q: What was one of the most difficult times in your life?

A: We spent three years, 1942-1945 operating a cattle ranch in Ruby Valley, Nevada, where Steve learned to mend fences, put up hay, feed cattle in the winter and sell them the next fall. HARD WORK!! I learned to cook three meals a day for twenty ravenous hay hands during haying season. There was no rural electricity in the valley but we had a little Delco system that generated enough power for lights, not enough to heat an electric iron so I heated the old fashioned flat irons on our coal kitchen range, churned butter, baked bread and many household duties. We didn't get to church during those years. The nearest branch was in Wells, fifty miles away, and cattle had to be fed seven days a week. We had two tiny little boys at that time, the younger one being five months old. Had he not had a beautiful disposition, I could not have survived.

Q: Tell me about your most memorable church calling.

A: In 1960 we were called to preside over the West German Mission in Duesseldorf, Germany. Steve, our oldest son was a few months shy of being missionary age so he served a mission himself to Austria. The other four children came with us and attended German schools. When we stepped off the plane in Duesseldorf, Steve stopped speaking English. He made a rule that only German would be spoken in the mission home and office. At that time wives of mission presidents were responsible for any call their husbands issued to them. Mine put me immediately to work as Mission Relief Society President. He refused to give me a missionary to translate for me and I leaned through study and reading and working side by side of my desk with the sister I called to be my counselor. She spoke no English, and I no German, but the spirit and love were there and we somehow communicated. Within a year I was understanding and speaking German. The members didn't mind that I made mistakes. They loved us for making the effort to learn their language. To this day I still say my prayers in German.

Question:

*I love working on my family history, but I tend
to work on pages in a random sort of fashion. What's the
best way for me to organize my random pages?*

It's important to work with what you have and to approach your family history in a way that works for you. I like to keep binders so I can easily add photographs and information as I find them. Because I use this system, I'm not afraid to scrapbook pages out of order, and my seemingly "random" pages really do have a home.

Take a peek at the first three chapters of this book and decide how you want to organize your photographs and documents, and what approach you want to take in scrapbooking them. I'll bet you'll find there's room to scrapbook in a random sort of way within a structure you've developed for yourself.

service in the
NAVY
during world war II

Jacob enlisted in the Navy, entering at the age of 18 years old (5.19.1943). His honorable discharge was less than 3 years later (1.28.1946). These are his handwritten notes to his sweetheart, Esther, on the backs of photographs taken of him during his time in the Navy.

Question:
I love creating scrapbook pages but must admit that journaling is my least favorite part of scrapbooking. Is it really necessary to journal on my family history pages? Or is it okay to just include a title, names and dates?

Take a look at the layouts featured at right. You'll notice that one has a lot of journaling, which gives insight into how my grandma was a delightful and funny girl. The other page (also the same grandma) has no journaling at all. We all want to read interesting facts and stories about our ancestors. Do your best. But once in a while, you'll come across a photograph of a relative that simply doesn't warrant specific details. That's okay!

I strongly encourage you to journal on your family history layouts. It's true— sometimes, you won't know the stories behind the pictures or you might not have much information to share. But if you can take a few moments and record what you do know, your future generations will thank you.

If journaling is difficult for you, consider the following two ways to make it a bit easier:

* Set aside a period of time to just work on blocks of journaling. Set up a standard journaling template on your computer. Copy it and paste it into your document. Type your journaling inside each block, print the blocks onto cardstock, cut them out and attach them to your layouts.

* Look for fun approaches to take with your journaling. Consider a bulleted list, a Q&A format, or even a simple who, what, where, when, why and how approach. Find something that really works for you and make it your journaling trademark in your family history albums.

Isn't she lovely?

ESTHER'S CHILDHOOD

When I asked Wendall (her younger brother by 2 years) to describe Esther as a girl growing up, he was quick to respond that she was your typical redhead.

Feisty, quick, sharp, lively, alert.

PHYSICAL FEATURES
My hair was orange and I had lots of freckles and I certainly had the temper to go with these! My mother and father both had red hair, so what else could I have? As I grew up I hated my hair, my freckles, my name, and the house we lived in. It was green.

MY NAMESAKE
I was named after my two grandmothers: Susan **Esther** Dean Jones and Sarah **Charity** Boyd Marion. I wanted names like everyone else – Ann, Mary, or Betty. But oh, how I learned to love those names as I reached maturity. To be named after my grandmothers!

FAVORITE TOYS
As a toddler I was a happy little girl. I have pictures of me playing with my favorite "toys", a tin cup and the woodpile. I would play for hours with my sticks. My father worked in the furniture factory and my wood was special – some with curves, some shiny, and they were a lot of fun. When we would kill our hogs, we children got the bladder and used it for our football.

LIVING DURING THE DEPRESSION
I remember the depression very clearly. I didn't know how poor we were until I grew up. Part of the time my father couldn't even get work so my eldest sister (14 years older than I) quit school and got a job in the sweater mills. Her first paycheck of 75 cents got corn meal and some of the necessities to eat.

OUR HOME
We only had one spigot in our house and our water had to be heated in a tub on the wood cook stove. On Saturday night we all got baths in the washtub. We only had an outside toilet. Each of our four rooms had one light hanging from the ceiling. We children would do our homework beside the fireplace. Of course we would burn on one side while the other side of us would be freezing. The bed I slept on had straw for a mattress and I'm afraid it actually had "bed bugs".

THE FAMILY CAR
My father got his one and only car the day I was born. Someone had to get outside and turn the crank to get it started. It was a '29 Chevrolet.

A RESOURCEFUL FAMILY
We always had big gardens and Mama always canned. We had chickens, cows, pigs, ducks, fruit and walnut trees, so we were a lot better off than a lot of people. Quite a few years we raised big fields of peanuts. After we would harvest the peanuts we had to spread them out in a spare room to dry. My mother always knew I would sneak into them because my mouth would get real sore.

GIVING WHAT LITTLE WE HAD
Our house was not too far from the railroad tracks and "beggars" used to get off the train and come by our house begging for food. My mama always shared. I remember one man that I just stood and stared at. His shoes had holes, his gloves had no fingers and his beard had ice and snow all over it. He sat in front of the fireplace and ate milk and cornbread (that's what we'd had) and was sure thankful for it. That night he slept in our stable with our cow.

CLOTHING & SHOES
My daddy would "mend" our shoes. After we would walk a while with cardboard in our shoes he would get some leather from somewhere and put a new sole on our shoes. I was so proud of these because I wouldn't be walking in rain and snow that would come though the holes. Mama had to do our washing in a big black pot in the yard. Later on she even had a scrub board.

MAKING MILK & BUTTER
Since we had a cow we had milk and butter. Of course to get the butter we had to churn. Oh, I hated that! We had two kinds of churns. One of them had the dash going up and down and the other, the wheel had to be pushed around. It seemed it would take hours to make the butter. But it was so good.

HOMEMAKING SKILLS
I learned to sew on a pedal sewing machine very young. My mama always made all our clothes so I was taught to do that. Even now my sewing machine and I are real good "friends". I have my grandmother's first "Singer" that is over a hundred and ten years old (this was written in 1996) and it still works well. All the ironing was done with a black "flat iron" that had to be heated on the wood cook stove.

TRADITIONS
Every Christmas we would sit around the fire place in a bedroom and crack out black walnuts so Mama could make some cakes for the holiday. These were always stored in our "pie safe" and the smell was out of this world! Our Christmas trees were usually cut down out of the pasture. They were usually put on our front porch because we had candles on them. Of course we children cut up pretty paper strips and put them together with "paste" glue. Most of the things we got were things my mama and papa made for us. Every year a man in town gave us a bag of oranges. Papa would buy us a box of stick candy. He would cut a hole in the top of the orange and we'd suck the juice from the orange through the candy. Oh, it was good (I still do this once in a while)!

All of this is taken from Esther's handwritten memoirs in February 1996.

{ **Question:**
How can I tell my family story in an interesting way?
I don't want my journaling to be boring or
trite—this is important stuff! }

Remember high-school English? Hang in here with me, okay? One of my assignments was to write an essay that compared and contrasted two objects. Well, journaling isn't exactly high-school English, but the time-tested "compare and contrast" method can help you tell your stories in an interesting way, like the page I created at right about the different experiences we had with the birth of our two children.

Family history really comes to light, for example, when we compare and contrast things like:

✱ *Transportation.* Did your grandmother walk to school? Did your mom ride the bus? Did you ride in a carpool?

✱ *Styles.* Did your grandmother wear a poodle skirt in high school? Did you wear a mini skirt in high school?

✱ *Music.* A friend's grandparents got dressed up and went swing dancing almost every weekend, but she's never gone to a dance with her husband (they prefer to fill their home with jazz melodies uploaded to their iPod!).

Do you see what I mean? You can compare and contrast almost anything in history to the way things are today, and I'll bet you'll enjoy seeing the differences between lifestyles. Just imagine how much your children's children will enjoy revisiting these pages again and again!

Compare
and Contrast
The births of Porter & Claire

Porter Wayne Higgins
12.3.02

Weather: Cold & snowy December afternoon

Labor length: 33 hours

Labor experience: Come & go labor, painful, dilated to 9 cm with no epidural, unsettling near the end

Delivery: Last-minute C-section (he was breech & we didn't know until time for delivery)

Newborn size: Little (6 lbs. 8 oz. and 18" long)

Mom's recovery: Difficult; scar tender for a LONG time

Dad's preparation for birth: Well rested; had vacation for several days before

Feelings about new addition: Overjoyed and extremely blessed

Claire Esther Higgins
9.20.05

Weather: Warm & sunny, beautiful September morning

Labor length: 7 hours

Labor experience: Induced early in the morning, controlled and calm. Grandma was there hanging out with us most of the time.

Delivery: VBAC

Newborn size: Big (9 lbs. and 20 ½" long)

Mom's recovery: MUCH better and quicker!

Dad's preparation for birth: On-call the night before at Metro Hospital and tired.

Feelings about new addition: Overjoyed and extremely blessed all over again

GOOD
MEMORIES

1979

we love naps.
(and quiet time)

we love to record our memories

we love to hang out with Simon.

christmas at the ranch (pendleton)

mom and me : chu OT 2005

2005

we love coffee.
(black, please)

we love each other

i love you.

we love not being in a hurry and taking our time

WONDERFULLY MADE

TRIBUTE ALBUM

Question:

*Can you share some tips on how to create
a family history gift album?*

A family history album can really be a cherished gift. You may be interested in creating an album that celebrates a wedding anniversary or that documents a retiree's career. Whatever project you choose to create, it's always a good idea to select a simple design scheme, add journaling that comes from your heart and, whenever possible, ask other people in your family to contribute photographs, memories and ideas.

A gift album doesn't have to be "old" stuff, either. Try paying tribute to a specific family relationship (I made this album for my sister-in-law and close friend a few years ago).

❧

{ **Question:**
I come from a long line of crafting women who loved to quilt, knit and crochet. How can I preserve their handiwork in my family history projects? }

I'll bet many scrapbookers have women who crafted in their family histories. If you have a framed cross-stitch project from your great-grandmother or a special quilt from your aunt, it's wonderful to include a photograph of these items on your scrapbook pages. Believe it or not, you may even be able to put soft items, like a quilt, directly on your scanner and scan a sample to put on your pages.

If possible, see if you can capture a macro (close-up) shot of the handcrafted item to include on your page. I'm constantly amazed at the tiny and precise stitches I see on my ancestors' projects (hand-stitching, no less!). My mom took a close-up shot of a quilt square on which my great-great "Grannie Jones" had stitched her name and age. Talk about priceless information!

When including these items on your pages, be sure to capture the stories behind the items too. For example, how long did it take your grandmother to complete a quilt? Where did she learn to quilt? Did she quilt by herself or with a group of friends? How many quilts did she make in her lifetime? Where did she find supplies to make each quilt? Did she have a favorite quilt, and if so, what was it?

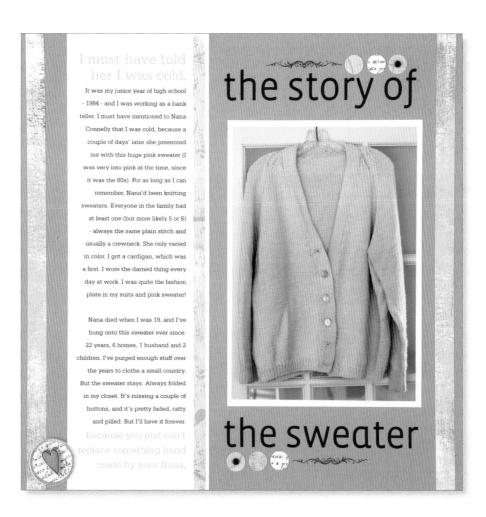

the story of

I must have told her I was cold.

It was my junior year of high school - 1984 - and I was working as a bank teller. I must have mentioned to Nana Connelly that I was cold, because a couple of days' later she presented me with this huge pink sweater (I was very into pink at the time, since it was the 80s). For as long as I can remember, Nana'd been knitting sweaters. Everyone in the family had at least one (but more likely 5 or 6) - always the same plain stitch and usually a crewneck. She only varied in color. I got a cardigan, which was a first. I wore the darned thing every day at work. I was quite the fashion plate in my suits and pink sweater!

Nana died when I was 19, and I've hung onto this sweater ever since. 22 years, 6 homes, 1 husband and 2 children. I've purged enough stuff over the years to clothe a small country. But the sweater stays. Always folded in my closet. It's missing a couple of buttons, and it's pretty faded, ratty and pilled. But I'll have it forever. Because you just can't replace something hand made by your Nana.

the sweater

Handiwork

BY GRANNY JONES

HANDIWORK N: A WORK PRODUCED BY HAND LABOR

IN THEIR DAY, IF YOU WANTED IT, YOU MADE IT. SO SUSAN MADE THE CLOTHES, THE BEDDING, AND ANYTHING THEY NEEDED. AMONG HER MANY QUILTS, THIS WAS ONE OF THE LAST ONES SHE MADE BEFORE SHE DIED. SHE ACTUALLY JUST MADE THE QUILT TOP AND HER GRANDDAUGHTER ESTHER FINISHED THE QUILT LATER, ADDING THE BATTING AND BACKSIDE TO THE QUILT.

SIGNATURE READS:

SUSAN JONES
1946 – AGE 87

THIS WAS THE SAME YEAR HER DAUGHTER EMMA DIED.

Question:

*How do I deal with copyright issues
involved with copying old photographs?*

Photo developers often refuse to make copies of old photographs out of fear of infringing on copyright laws. So, it's only natural that you're worried!

If there's no information about a photograph, it can be difficult to determine who owns the copyright. However, if you know who took the photograph, then that person owns the copyright. Even if a person hires a wedding photographer, the photographer owns the copyright unless it's transferred in writing. Because many of the photographs you're scrapbooking will be older, the photographer may no longer be living. In this case, the rights of the photograph are determined by the photographer's will or given as personal property. Just ask permission of the owner to reproduce it.

If you're still concerned, visit *http://www.copyright.gov/fls/fl102.html* for more information.

Question:

*I've started asking family members for information
about our history, but I'm getting a lower response rate than
I'd hoped. Any tips on how I can increase participation?*

I've found that it's most effective to break things down into manageable bits. For example, ask someone to tell you one story about their childhood instead of saying, "I have 500 questions to ask you!" Also, people sometimes get worried when they hear the term "family history" and think you're going to try and rope them into a huge project. It's sometimes easier just to ask a question here and there in a very informal way.

Question:

*I inherited several magnetic albums from my
grandmother and the photographs are falling apart.
What's the best way to remove them from the albums?*

Unfortunately, many precious, timeless photographs were put into magnetic albums. The pages in these albums eat away at the backs of the photographs, meaning you can lose these treasures forever! So stop the deteriorating process now by trying some of these techniques:

1 Try dental floss. Use a sawing motion along the back of the photograph to remove it from the page.

2 Use a product designed specifically for removing photos from albums, like un-du (you can find it at scrapbooking or craft stores). It's completely safe for old photos.

3 Try a hot or cold method. Put the album page in the freezer to make the glue brittle, or use a microwave or hairdryer to loosen the glue.

Question:

*I have hundreds of miscellaneous family photographs,
but I don't feel I have enough photographs to
actually tell a story. What should I do?*

It's not uncommon to find tons of photographs but have no idea of the who, what or where that can be told from the pictures. Here are some ways to help:

1 Interview any family members you can. They may know who is in the photos and have memories to share.

2 If you know who is in the photo, write down anything you can remember about this person on the layout. Share your own memories.

3 If there is a date on the back of the photo, just add information about that year (check the Internet for events, facts, etc). Include this information along with the photograph on your layout.

ONCE UPON
A TIME...

...there was
a little
girl with
curls in her
hair and
everyone
LOVED
her.

 Geneva

1946. Geneva. That is all that my grandma wrote on the back of this photo. I am so glad she wrote on all the photos. It helps me to identify people & sometimes places, but, geez, I wish she had written more from time to time. There are many reasons why I love this photo: my aunt is adorable, the chickens are cute, and strangely enough, I love this photo because it reminds me of why I started scrapbooking. I started it to do more than identify people. I did it to remember. I wish I knew why Geneva had all that interesting looking jewelry on. I wish I knew which farm she was at & I wish I knew some of the things she said that day. I am so lucky to have this darling photo to remind me of the beauty of preserving ones memories.

W hen looking through my heritage photos, I love looking at the images of my relatives as children. But one thing that always poses a problem for me is that either the photo has no identifying information or there are just the basic facts written in pen on the back. I decided to create a childhood heritage album that incorporates these photos and my own personal style. Here's the process I followed to create my family history album.

1. GATHER. I asked my relatives to send me their favorite childhood photographs.

2. SORT. I selected one favorite photograph of each relative.

3. PREPARE/ORGANIZE. I decided to scrapbook just one photograph of each person. On the corresponding page of each layout, I wrote about how each photograph makes me feel and how it reflects each person's personality.

4. DISCOVER. To complete my layouts, I discovered additional details about each subjects' life story.

5. PRESENT. Fun colors, creative journaling and graphic design represent my scrapbooking style, so I used all of those elements in my scrapbook.

—*Carey Johnson*

T really love this idea and hope you will, too! For this project, I created a fill-in-the-blank autobiography. This book can be completed by the recipient as she has time, and because I used fill-in-the-blank questions, the questions are very user-friendly. You can make a similar project in just a few easy steps:

1. Choose an album for your project.

2. On your computer, set up a list of fill-in-the-blank questions.

3. Print out the questions.

4. Decorate the printed question pages.

5. If desired, add pockets or places where the recipient can slip in photographs or documents.

6. Slip the finished pages into sheet protectors.

Sketches

Looking for simple
and classic layout designs
for scrapbooking
your family history?

These sketches are a great starting point

for creating timeless layouts that showcase your

family stories and photographs. These ideas

can easily be adapted to two-page layouts or

transferred to your 12" x 12" scrapbook pages.

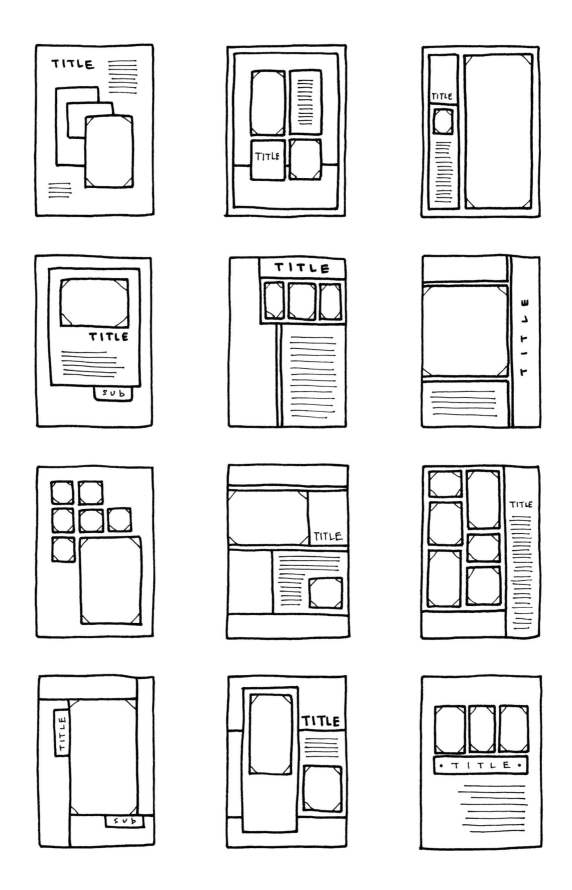

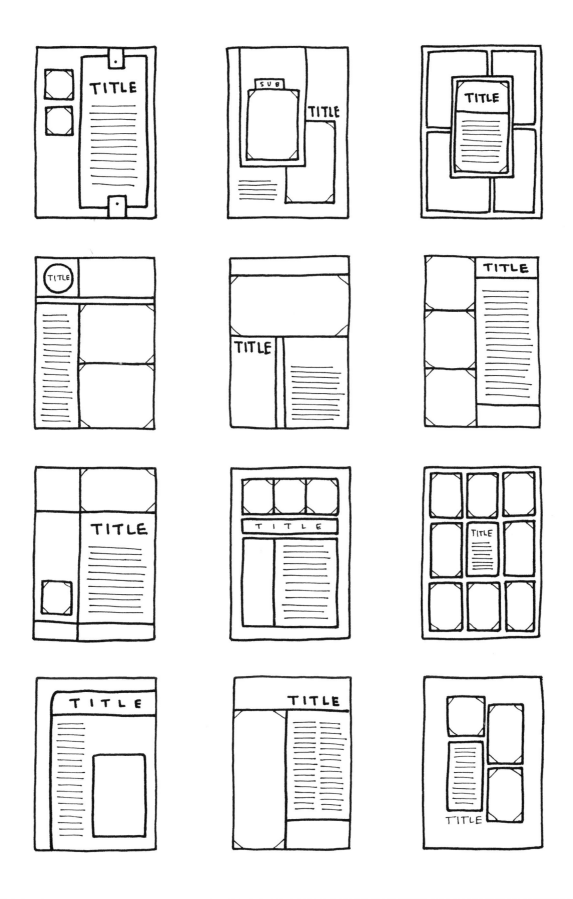

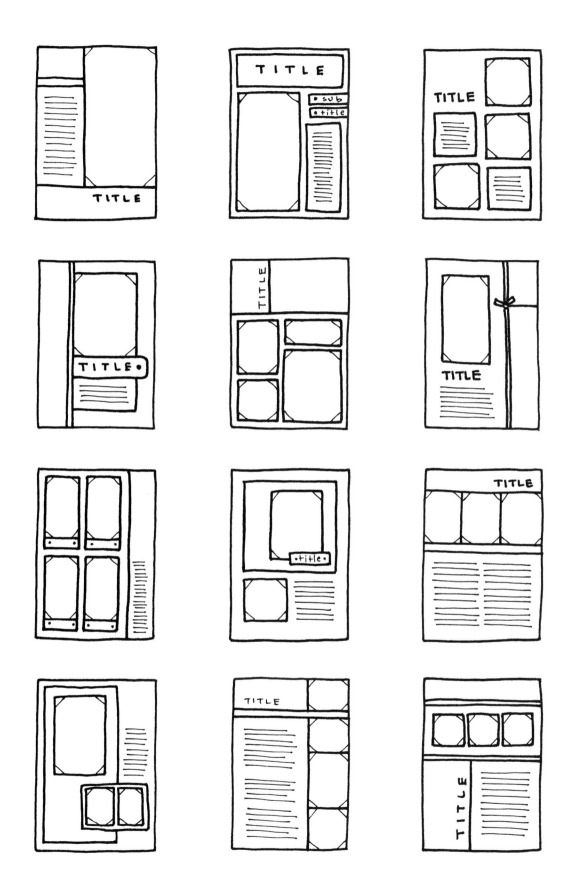

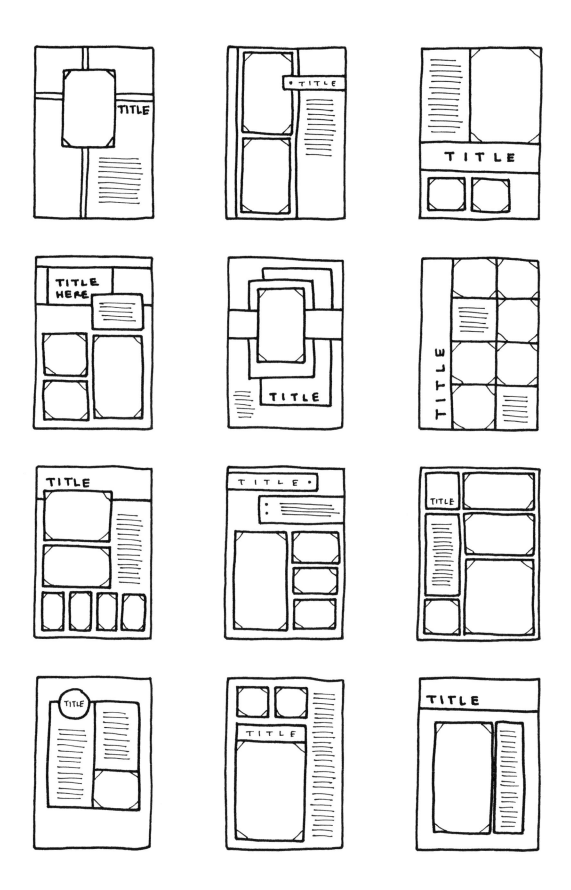

  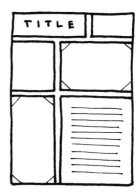

Introduction

p. 5

ESTHER, THE HOMEMAKER *by Becky Higgins* SUPPLIES *Cardstock:*
Bazzill Basics Paper; *Ribbon:* SEI; *Paper flowers:* Prima; *Brad:* Lasting
Impressions for Paper; *Corner-rounder punch:* EK Success; *Computer font:*
Garamond, downloaded from the Internet.

p. 7

ROY *by Becky Higgins* SUPPLIES *Cardstock:* Bazzill Basics Paper; *Page pebble:* Making Memories; *Computer fonts:* Xband Rough ("Roy"), Zurich Extra
Condensed BT (subtitles) and Abadi MT Condensed Light (journaling), downloaded from the Internet.

IN HER KITCHEN *by Becky Higgins* SUPPLIES *Cardstock:* Bazzill Basics
Paper; *Patterned paper:* K&Company; *Corner-rounder and circle punches:*
EK Success; *Brads:* Lasting Impressions for Paper; *Computer font:*
SimplexLight, downloaded from the Internet.

Chapter 1

p. 8

STEWART BROTHERS *by Becky Higgins* SUPPLIES *Cardstock:* Bazzill
Basics Paper; *Patterned paper:* My Mind's Eye; *Computer font:* Rockwell,
package unknown; *Other:* Thread.

p. 17

EVERYTHING *by April Peterson* SUPPLIES *Patterned papers:* KI Memories
and Autumn Leaves; *Chipboard:* Fancy Pants Design; *Die cut:* KI Memories;
Computer font: Batang, downloaded from the Internet.

SCHOOL LIFE *by Becky Higgins* SUPPLIES *Cardstock:* Bazzill Basics Paper;
Patterned paper: Karen Foster Design; *Bookplate die cut:* Sizzix, Provo
Craft; *Brads:* Making Memories; *Computer fonts:* CrudFont (title), Andale
Mono (questions) and Garamond (answers), downloaded from the Internet;
Other: Thread.

p. 19

CONNELLY *by Lisa Russo* SUPPLIES *Patterned paper:* Autumn Leaves;
Flower: Doodlebug Design; *Clear buttons:* 7gypsies; *Gem:* Making
Memories; *Photo corners:* Canson; *Computer fonts:* Academia and
Blackjack, downloaded from the Internet.

LOVE STORY *by Becky Higgins* SUPPLIES *Cardstock:* Bazzill Basics Paper;
Patterned paper: Die Cuts With a View; *Bookplate:* Li'l Davis Designs;
Brads: All My Memories; *Photo corners:* 3L; *Computer font:* Times New
Roman, Microsoft Word.

p. 20

CHEROKEE HERITAGE? *by Becky Higgins* SUPPLIES *Computer font:* CK
Extra, "Fresh Fonts" CD, *Creating Keepsakes*.

SUPPLIES

p. 23

ANNIE & PEARLIE JONES *by Becky Higgins* SUPPLIES *Paper flowers:*
Prima; *Brads:* All My Memories; *Photo corners:* 3L; *Computer fonts:* CK
Elegant (title), "Fresh Fonts" CD, *Creating Keepsakes*; Skia (journaling), downloaded from the Internet.

p. 25

1925 *by Karen Russell* SUPPLIES *Patterned paper:* Prime Stamp Exchange;
Computer font: Modern #22, downloaded from the Internet; *Brads:* Making
Memories; *Punch:* Fiskars; *Other:* Acrylic paint.

BABY VICKI *by Becky Higgins* SUPPLIES *Patterned paper:* Chatterbox;
Ribbon: SEI; *Paper flower:* Prima; *Brad:* Karen Foster Design; *Photo corners:*
3L; *Corner-rounder punch:* EK Success; *Computer fonts:* CK Elegant
("Baby") and CK Chemistry, "Fresh Fonts" CD, *Creating Keepsakes*.

p. 26

BEAR ENCOUNTER *by Becky Higgins. Journaling by Dan Higgins.*
SUPPLIES *Patterned paper:* Chatterbox; *Brads:* Doodlebug Design; *Computer
font:* Gill Sans, downloaded from the Internet.

p. 29

P. E. CROUSHORN *by Becky Higgins* SUPPLIES *Cardstock:* Bazzill Basics
Paper; *Bookplate:* Making Memories; *Brads:* Die Cuts With a View; *Photo
corners:* Heidi Swapp for Advantus; *Computer font:* Clique-Serif, downloaded from the Internet.

MAHONRI: THE POET *by Becky Higgins* SUPPLIES *Patterned paper:*
Daisy D's Paper Co.; *Photo corners:* 3L; *Bookplate:* Li'l Davis Designs; *Brads:*
Making Memories; *Computer font:* Times New Roman, Microsoft Word.

p. 31

COPING *by Lisa Brown Caveney* SUPPLIES *Patterned paper:* Mustard
Moon; *Epoxy letters:* KI Memories.

ALMOST SISTERS *by Melissa Chapman* SUPPLIES *Cardstock:* Prism
Papers; *Patterned paper:* Scenic Route Paper Co.; *Flowers:* Making
Memories; *Photo turn:* Junkitz; *Brads:* Bazzill Basics Paper and Memory
Makers; *Rub-ons:* Paper House Productions; *Computer fonts:* Voluta and
Geosans Light, downloaded from the Internet.

p. 33

LOVE LETTERS *by Mimi Schramm* **SUPPLIES** *Cardstock:* Bazzill Basics Paper; *Patterned paper, bookplate and stickers:* K&Company; *Vellum:* The Paper Company; *Stamping ink:* Distress Ink, Ranger Industries; *Thread:* Coats & Clark; *Circle punch:* Marvy Uchida; *Brads:* Making Memories; *Elastic string:* Westrim Crafts; *Computer fonts:* MarnieRegular and Blackjack, downloaded from the Internet.

p. 34

FLASH CARDS *by Becky Higgins* **SUPPLIES** *Corner-rounder punch:* EK Success; *Computer font:* Rockwell, downloaded from the Internet.

p. 35

MEMORY GAME *by Becky Higgins* **SUPPLIES** *Patterned paper:* My Mind's Eye.

Chapter 2

p. 36

EMMA AND ME *by Becky Higgins* **SUPPLIES** *Cardstock:* Bazzill Basics Paper; *Paper flower:* Prima; *Photo corners:* 3L; *Brad:* Karen Foster Design; *Corner-rounder punch:* EK Success; *Computer font:* SimplexLight, downloaded from the Internet; *Other:* Thread.

p. 41

ADOLF AUGUST ALLGAIER *by Becky Higgins* **SUPPLIES** *Cardstock:* Bazzill Basics Paper; *Corner-rounder punch:* EK Success; *Computer fonts:* Badhouse Bold (title) and Swiss 721 Light Condensed BT (journaling), downloaded from the Internet.

IN HIS OWN WORDS *by Becky Higgins* **SUPPLIES** *Cardstock:* Bazzill Basics Paper; *Photo corners:* 3L; *Computer fonts:* Device (story titles) and American Typewriter (journaling), downloaded from the Internet.

p. 42

HURON COLLEGE *by Becky Higgins* **SUPPLIES** *Cardstock:* Bazzill Basics Paper; *Photo corners:* 3L; *Brads:* All My Memories; *Computer fonts:* Anastasia (title) and Amery Thin-Normal (journaling), downloaded from the Internet.

p. 45

WEDDING DAY *by Becky Higgins* **SUPPLIES** *Cardstock:* Bazzill Basics Paper; *Ribbon:* BasicGrey; *Paper flowers:* Prima; *Brads:* Die Cuts With a View; *Computer fonts:* CK Elegant (title), "Fresh Fonts" CD and CK Regal "Creative Clips & Fonts for Special Occasions" CD, Creating Keepsakes.

EARL'S RESUME IN 1932 *by Becky Higgins* **SUPPLIES** *Cardstock:* Bazzill Basics Paper; *Patterned paper:* BasicGrey; *Brads:* Die Cuts With a View; *Computer font:* Courier, downloaded from the Internet.

p. 46

ESTHER'S STUFF *by Becky Higgins* **SUPPLIES** *Cardstock:* Bazzill Basics Paper; *Paper flower:* Prima; *Brad:* Karen Foster Design; *Computer font:* Adramalech, downloaded from the Internet; *Other:* Thread.

p. 48

THE LETTER *by Becky Higgins* **SUPPLIES** *Cardstock:* Bazzill Basics Paper; *Computer font:* Rockwell, downloaded from the Internet.

p. 49

GRANDMA'S PIGS *by Carey Johnson* **SUPPLIES** *Software:* Adobe Photoshop, Adobe Systems; *Patterned paper:* Carolee's Creations; *Jewels:* Making Memories; *Computer font:* Courier, Microsoft Word; *Other:* Buttons.

p. 51

TINA LYNN WHITE *by Becky Higgins. Photos from Tina Johnson.* **SUPPLIES** *Cardstock:* Bazzill Basics Paper.

VANDERPOL *by Rachel Ludwig* **SUPPLIES** *Cardstock:* Bazzill Basics Paper; *Letter stickers and pen:* American Crafts; *Circle cutter:* Creative Memories.

p. 53

LOVE LETTERS *by Becky Higgins* **SUPPLIES** *Cardstock:* Bazzill Basics Paper; *Patterned paper:* My Mind's Eye; *Ribbon:* Making Memories; *Brads:* Die Cuts With a View; *Computer fonts:* CK Elegant (title), "Fresh Fonts" CD, Creating Keepsakes; Angelus, downloaded from the Internet.

WRITE *by Carey Johnson* **SUPPLIES** *Patterned paper and chipboard letters:* Scenic Route Paper Co.; *Star:* Heidi Swapp for Advantus; *Computer font:* Century Gothic, Microsoft Word.

p. 56

ASHER BOOK OF MEMORIES *by Jen Lehmann* **SUPPLIES** *Patterned paper:* Michaels; *Chalk:* Deluxe Cuts; *Charms:* Darice; *Ribbon:* Jo-Ann Stores.

p. 57

KOREAN WAR *by Jen Lehmann* **SUPPLIES** *Patterned papers:* Rusty Pickle and Karen Foster Design.

p. 58

COLLAGE OF COUPLES *by Becky Higgins*

Chapter 3

p. 60

THE CARLSON FAMILY *by Becky Higgins* **SUPPLIES** *Patterned papers and letter "C":* BasicGrey; *Computer font:* Times New Roman, Microsoft.

p. 63

WEDDING RECEPTION *by Becky Higgins* **SUPPLIES** *Cardstock:* Bazzill Basics Paper; *Patterned paper:* Chatterbox; *Photo corners:* 3L; *Paper flowers:* Prima; *Brads:* K&Company (pearl) and Doodlebug Design (gray); *Computer font:* Garamond, downloaded from the Internet.

p. 65

NAVY *by Kerri Bradford* **SUPPLIES** *Patterned paper:* Paper Loft; *Acetate frame and star:* Heidi Swapp for Advantus; *Chipboard letters:* Pressed Petals; *Numbers:* Prime Stamp Exchange; *Acrylic paint:* Americana Paints, DecoArt; *Stamping ink:* StazOn, Tsukineko; *Index tab:* Avery.

THEIR STORY *by Becky Higgins* **SUPPLIES** *Cardstock:* Bazzill Basics Paper; *Photo corners:* 3L; *Brads:* Conectics; *Computer fonts:* CK Elegant (title), "Fresh Fonts" CD, Creating Keepsakes; Garamond (journaling), downloaded from the Internet.

p. 66

PRETTY AS A PRINCESS *by Becky Higgins* **SUPPLIES** *Cardstock:* Bazzill Basics Paper; *Paper flower:* Prima; *Photo corners:* 3L; *Large brad:* Karen Foster Design; *Computer fonts:* Omatic (title) and Skia (journaling), downloaded from the Internet.

p. 69

WWII *by Becky Higgins* **SUPPLIES** *Cardstock:* Bazzill Basics Paper; *Computer font:* Rockwell, downloaded from the Internet; *Other:* Thread.

p. 71

OUR LDS ROOTS *by Becky Higgins* **SUPPLIES** *Cardstock:* Bazzill Basics Paper; *Patterned paper:* K&Company; *Computer fonts:* Garamond, downloaded from the Internet; CK Elegant, "Fresh Fonts" CD, Creating Keepsakes; *Other:* Thread.

p. 73

LEARNING TO DRIVE *by Becky Higgins* **SUPPLIES** *Cardstock:* Bazzill Basics Paper; *Patterned papers:* Daisy D's Paper Co.; *Photo corners:* 3L; *Computer font:* Verdana, downloaded from the Internet.

FAMILY OF FARMERS *by Joy Uzarraga* **SUPPLIES** *Cardstock:* Bazzill Basics Paper; *Patterned paper and letter stickers:* BasicGrey; *Paper trees:* Jolee's by You, EK Success; *Computer fonts:* Garamond, Monotype Typography.

p. 74

MODEL A FORD *by Becky Higgins* **SUPPLIES** *Cardstock:* Bazzill Basics Paper; *Corner-rounder punch:* EK Success; *Computer fonts:* Badhouse Bold (title) and Avant Garde (journaling), downloaded from the Internet.

p. 77

YORKVILLE HIGH SCHOOL *by Becky Higgins* **SUPPLIES** *Cardstock:* Bazzill Basics Paper; *Patterned paper:* Chatterbox; *Photo corners:* 3L; *Paper flower:* Prima; *Brads:* Lasting Impressions for Paper; *Computer font:* Clique-Serif, downloaded from the Internet.

MEMORABILIA POCKET *by Loni Stevens* SUPPLIES *Patterned paper:* Scenic Route Paper Co.; *Magnetic closures:* BasicGrey; *Snap:* Making Memories; *Computer fonts:* Times New Roman, Microsoft Word; Italic and Quick Type, downloaded from the Internet; *Other:* Vellum.

p. 78
RECIPE BOX *by Becky Higgins* SUPPLIES *Cardstock:* Bazzill Basics Paper; *Patterned paper:* BasicGrey; *Corner-rounder punch:* EK Success; *Computer fonts:* Impact, downloaded from the Internet; Century Gothic, Microsoft Word.

p. 81
MAX *by Kerri Bradford* SUPPLIES *Patterned papers:* My Mind's Eye and BasicGrey; *Transparencies:* Creative Imaginations; *Rub-on designs:* My Mind's Eye; *Rub-on letters:* Heidi Swapp for Advantus; *Ribbon:* May Arts, Li'l Davis Designs, Making Memories and Paper Daisy; *Ribbon charm and brads:* Making Memories; *Tags:* Rusty Pickle; *Letter stamps:* Ma Vinci's Reliquary; *Embossing powder:* Stampendous!; *Preprinted pocket and photo anchor:* 7gypsies; *Label tape:* Dymo; *Stamping ink:* StazOn, Tsukineko; ColorBox Fluid Chalk, Clearsnap; *Other:* Silk flowers and eyelets.

p. 83
FAMILY STORYBOOK *by Becky Higgins* SUPPLIES *Album:* K&Company; *Textured cardstock:* Bazzill Basics Paper; *Photo corners:* 3L; *Brads:* Boxer Scrapbook Productions; *Circle punches:* EK Success; *Computer font:* Futura, downloaded from the Internet.

Chapter 4

p. 84
THE FUN SIDE OF ESTHER *by Becky Higgins* SUPPLIES *Cardstock:* Bazzill Basics Paper; *Ribbon:* SEI; *Photo corners:* 3L; *Computer font:* Verdana, downloaded from the Internet.

p. 89
JUST DESERTS *by Kerri Bradford* SUPPLIES *Patterned papers:* BasicGrey and Chatterbox; *Chipboard letters:* Pressed Petals; *Buckle and file folder:* Rusty Pickle; *Ribbon:* Chatterbox; *Stamping ink:* ColorBox Fluid Chalk, Clearsnap; *Computer font:* CAC Shishoni Brush, downloaded from *www.twopeasinabucket.com.*

HANDWRITTEN RECIPES *by Becky Higgins* SUPPLIES *Cardstock:* Bazzill Basics Paper; *Patterned paper:* Chatterbox; *Chipboard bookplates:* Heidi Swapp for Advantus; *Brads:* Bazzill Basics Paper (small green), Making Memories (large orange); *Computer font:* Garamond, downloaded from the Internet.

p. 91
BIRTHDAY GIRL *by Becky Higgins* SUPPLIES *Cardstock:* Bazzill Basics Paper; *Paper flowers:* Prima; *Brads:* Jo-Ann Scrap Essentials (large); Die Cuts With a View (small); *Computer fonts:* Century Gothic, Microsoft Word; CK Elegant, "Fresh Fonts" CD, *Creating Keepsakes; Other:* Thread.

PRODIGAL DAUGHTER *by Beth Opel* SUPPLIES *Textured cardstock:* Bazzill Basics Paper and Prism Papers; *Patterned papers:* Anna Griffin and Paper Salon; *Brads:* Making Memories; *Metal letters:* American Crafts; *Crocheted flowers and ribbon:* SEI; *Rickrack:* Creative Impressions; *Metal word disc:* KI Memories; *Deacidification spray:* Archival Mist, Preservation Technologies; *Computer font:* Times New Roman, Microsoft Word.

p. 93
MY AUNT KATIE *by Lisa Bearnson* SUPPLIES *Patterned paper:* Chatterbox; *Flowers:* Making Memories; *Stamping ink:* ColorBox, Clearsnap; *Chalk:* Craf-T Products; *Letters:* Heidi Swapp for Advantus; *Decorative-edged scissors:* Fiskars.

MEMORIES OF GRANDPA *by Becky Higgins, Journaling and Photos by Sabrina Atwood* SUPPLIES *Cardstock:* Bazzill Basics Paper; *Page pebbles:* Making Memories; *Brads:* Lasting Impressions for Paper; *Computer font:* Skia, downloaded from the Internet; *Other:* Thread.

p. 95
THE END OF EMMA MARION'S LIFE *by Becky Higgins* SUPPLIES *Cardstock:* Bazzill Basics Paper; *Paper flower:* Prima; *Brads:* Lasting Impressions for Paper; *Computer fonts:* CK Elegant, "Fresh Fonts" CD, *Creating Keepsakes;* Abadi MT Condensed Light, downloaded from the Internet; *Other:* Thread.

EMMA'S DEATH *by Becky Higgins* SUPPLIES *Cardstock:* Bazzill Basics Paper; *Patterned paper:* Daisy D's Paper Co.; *Computer font:* CK Chemistry, "Fresh Fonts" CD, *Creating Keepsakes.*

p. 97
HARTMAN'S STUDIO *by Carey Johnson* SUPPLIES *Patterned paper:* Scenic Route Paper Co.; *Sticker:* American Crafts; *Cardstock circle:* Technique Tuesday; *Computer fonts:* 2Peas You Are There and 2Peas Airplane, downloaded from *www.twopeasinabucket.com;* Century Gothic, Microsoft Word; Jokewood, downloaded from the Internet.

MOTHERS AND DAUGHTERS *by Becky Higgins* SUPPLIES *Cardstock:* Bazzill Basics Paper; *Patterned paper:* 7gypsies; *Brads:* All My Memories; *Photo corners:* Heidi Swapp for Advantus; *Computer fonts:* SuburbanLight (names) and Abadi MT Condensed Light (journaling), downloaded from the Internet.

p. 101
ELSIE AS ALICE *by Jamie Waters* SUPPLIES *Patterned papers:* Autumn Leaves and Crate Paper; *Buttons:* Autumn Leaves; *Letter stickers:* Doodlebug Design; *Sticker strip:* Pebbles Inc.; *Computer font:* American Typewriter, downloaded from the Internet; *Pen:* American Crafts.

EARL'S CAREER IN PICTURES *by Becky Higgins* SUPPLIES *Cardstock:* Bazzill Basics Paper; *Brads:* All My Memories; *Computer fonts:* Compacta Light BT (title), downloaded from the Internet; Times New Roman, Microsoft Word.

p. 103
BE ACTIVE *by Carey Johnson* SUPPLIES *Patterned paper and chipboard letters:* Scenic Route Paper Co.; *Stickers:* American Crafts; *Brad:* Ensemble by Brandy; *Computer font:* Courier New, Microsoft Word.

HIS WORK *by Becky Higgins* SUPPLIES *Cardstock:* Bazzill Basics Paper; *Computer font:* Andale Mono, downloaded from the Internet.

p. 104
QUESTIONS *by Becky Higgins* SUPPLIES *Patterned paper:* Anna Griffin; *Computer font:* Garamond, downloaded from the Internet.

p. 107
80 *by Tori Howell* SUPPLIES *Album:* Chatterbox; *Textured cardstock:* Die Cuts With a View; *Ribbon:* C.M. Offray & Son; *Bookplate, frame and brads:* Making Memories; *Computer fonts:* Bradley, downloaded from the Internet; Century Gothic, Microsoft Word; *Other:* Patterned paper.

Chapter 5

p. 110
SCHOOL FOR CARL *by Becky Higgins* SUPPLIES *Textured cardstock:* Bazzill Basics Paper; *Patterned paper:* Daisy D's Paper Co.; *Photo corners:* 3L; *Arrow:* 7gypsies; *Brad:* Die Cuts With a View; *Computer font:* Courier, downloaded from the Internet.

p.113
CONTENTS *by Jamie Waters* SUPPLIES *Patterned paper:* Crate Paper; *Chipboard letters:* Heidi Swapp for Advantus; *Bookplate:* Li'l Davis Designs; *Pen:* American Crafts: *Flower:* Prima; *Computer font:* 2Peas Weathered Fence, downloaded from *www.twopeasinabucket.com.*

HIGGINS & FOOTE *by Becky Higgins* SUPPLIES *Textured cardstock:* Bazzill Basics Paper; *Computer font:* Clique-Serif, downloaded from the Internet.

p. 114
GRADUATION *by Becky Higgins* SUPPLIES *Textured cardstock:* Bazzill Basics Paper; *Photo corners:* 3L; *Computer font:* Garamond, downloaded from the Internet.

p. 119
COLLEGE *by Carey Johnson* SUPPLIES *Software:* Adobe Photoshop, Adobe Systems; *Computer font:* Courier New, Microsoft Word.

CHURCH SERVICE *by Becky Higgins* SUPPLIES *Textured cardstock:* Bazzill Basics Paper; *Patterned paper:* K&Company; *Circle and corner-rounder punches:* EK Success; *Computer font:* CK Regal, "Creative Clips & Fonts for Special Occasions" CD, *Creating Keepsakes.*

p.121

THE EARLY DAYS *by Becky Higgins* SUPPLIES *Textured cardstock:* Bazzill Basics Paper; *Patterned paper:* Crate Paper; *Paper flower:* Prima; *Page pebble:* Making Memories; *Brad:* Lasting Impressions for Paper; *Computer font:* CK Constitution, "Fresh Fonts" CD, *Creating Keepsakes; Other:* Thread.

READING, WRITING AND SINGING *by Lisa Russo* SUPPLIES *Patterned papers:* Crate Paper and KI Memories; *Acrylic letter:* Autumn Leaves; *Transparency:* Creative Imaginations; *Brads:* American Crafts; *Computer fonts:* VistaSansLight, AdageScript, Classic Type and AdineKernberg, downloaded from the Internet.

p. 123

TROY *by Becky Higgins* SUPPLIES *Cardstock:* Bazzill Basics Paper; *Patterned paper:* Craft; *Photo corners:* 3L; *Computer font:* CK Newsprint, "Fresh Fonts" CD, *Creating Keepsakes.*

p. 125

JAKE & ESTHER JOHNSON'S FARM *by Becky Higgins* SUPPLIES *Cardstock:* Bazzill Basics Paper; *Brads:* All My Memories; *Photo corners:* Heidi Swapp for Advantus; *Computer font:* Rockwell, downloaded from the Internet.

PICNICS AT THE FARM *by Becky Higgins* SUPPLIES *Cardstock:* Bazzill Basics Paper; *Brads:* All My Memories; *Photo corners:* Heidi Swapp for Advantus; *Computer fonts:* Rockwell (titles) and Century Gothic, downloaded from the Internet; *Other:* Thread.

p. 127

MARJORIE ESTHER BRAND STEWART *by Becky Higgins* SUPPLIES *Cardstock:* Bazzill Basics Paper; *Brads:* Making Memories; *Computer font:* Garamond, downloaded from the Internet; *Other:* Thread.

ORSON & TILLIE FOOTE *by Becky Higgins* SUPPLIES *Textured cardstock:* Bazzill Basics Paper; *Brads:* Making Memories; *Computer font:* Garamond, downloaded from the Internet; *Other:* Thread.

p. 129

MARZ AND FISCHER *by Becky Higgins* SUPPLIES *Album and brads:* Making Memories; *Textured cardstock:* Bazzill Basics Paper; *Patterned paper:* K&Company; *Photo corners:* 3L; *Computer fonts:* CK Typewriter, "Fresh Fonts" CD, *Creating Keepsakes;* Abadi MT Condensed Light, downloaded from the Internet; *Other:* Thread.

FAMILY ALBUM *by Joanna Bolick* SUPPLIES *Patterned papers:* Chatterbox, Anna Griffin, My Mind's Eye and Scenic Route Paper Co.; *Chipboard letters and journaling sticky note:* Heidi Swapp for Advantus; *Pen:* Pigma Micron, Sakura; *Other:* Typewriter.

p. 131

JOHAN MARTIN ALLGAIER *by Becky Higgins* SUPPLIES *Cardstock:* Bazzill Basics Paper; *Patterned paper:* BasicGrey; *Photo corners:* Heidi Swapp for Advantus; *Computer font:* Angelus, downloaded from the Internet.

MELY'S 40TH *by Joy Uzarraga* SUPPLIES *Cardstock:* Bazzill Basics Paper; *Patterned paper:* BasicGrey; *Paper flowers:* Prima; *Brads:* American Crafts; *Computer font:* Gill Sans, Monotype Corporation; *Pen:* Gelly Roll, Sakura.

p.133

WHAT'S IN A NAME? *by Laurie Scholzen* SUPPLIES *Album:* Colorbök; *Patterned paper:* K&Company; *Brads:* Doodlebug Design; *Ribbon:* American Crafts (brown) and C.M. Offray & Son (pink); *Photo corners:* 3L; *Computer font:* Berlin ans FB, downloaded from the Internet; *Other:* Thread.

p.135

BRAG BOOK *by Becky Higgins* SUPPLIES *Album and foam letter stamps:* Making Memories; *Acrylic paint:* Plaid Enterprises; *Blue frame on cover:* Westrim Crafts; *Black circle letter stickers:* Li'l Davis Designs; *Computer font:* CK Stenography, "Fresh Fonts" CD, *Creating Keepsakes.*

Chapter 6

p. 137

WHO WAS HE? *by Becky Higgins* SUPPLIES *Cardstock:* Bazzill Basics Paper; *Brads:* Doodlebug Design; *Computer font:* Clique-Serif, downloaded from the Internet.

p. 139

BROTHERS *by Becky Higgins* SUPPLIES *Cardstock:* Bazzill Basics Paper; *Photo corners:* 3L; *Computer fonts:* Xband Rough (title) and Abadi MT Condensed Light (journaling), downloaded from the Internet.

SCHOOL PHOTOS *by Lisa Brown Caveney* SUPPLIES *Patterned paper:* Mustard Moon.

p. 141

CORRESPONDENCE *by Lisa Russo* SUPPLIES *Patterned paper:* Scenic Route Paper Co.; *Brads and letter stickers:* American Crafts; *String envelopes:* Two Peas in a Bucket; *Computer fonts:* American Gothic URW Light and Amethyst Script, downloaded from the Internet.

RUBY MAE OLESON RICHARDS *by Becky Higgins, Interview Journaling by Sarah Blamires* SUPPLIES *Cardstock:* Bazzill Basics Paper; *Patterned paper and borders:* K&Company; *Computer fonts:* CK Elegant (title), "Fresh Fonts" CD, *Creating Keepsakes;* American Typewriter (questions), downloaded from the Internet; Century Gothic (answers), Microsoft Word; *Other:* Thread.

p. 143

NAVY *by Becky Higgins* SUPPLIES *Cardstock:* Bazzill Basics Paper; *Photo corners:* 3L; *Computer fonts:* Dynamoehard (title) and Futura (journaling), downloaded from the Internet.

p. 145

ISN'T SHE LOVELY? *by Becky Higgins* SUPPLIES *Cardstock:* Bazzill Basics Paper; *Patterned paper:* K&Company; *Paper flowers:* Prima; *Brads:* Lasting Impressions for Paper; *Letter stamp:* Making Memories; *Acrylic paint:* Plaid Enterprises; *Corner-rounder punch:* Marvy Uchida.

ESTHER'S CHILDHOOD *by Becky Higgins* SUPPLIES *Patterned paper:* Chatterbox; *Photo corners:* 3L; *Corner-rounder punch:* Marvy Uchida; *Computer fonts:* CK Odd Ball (title), "Fresh Fonts" CD Vol. 2, *Creating Keepsakes;* Swis721 Light Condensed BT (journaling), downloaded from the Internet.

p. 147

COMPARE AND CONTRAST *by Becky Higgins* SUPPLIES *Patterned papers:* My Mind's Eye; *Bookplate and brad:* BasicGrey; *Circle and corner-rounder punches:* EK Success; *Computer fonts:* CK Elegant, "Fresh Fonts" CD, *Creating Keepsakes;* Abadi MT Condensed Light, downloaded from the Internet; *Other:* Thread.

GOOD MEMORIES *by Ali Edwards* SUPPLIES *Cardstock:* Bazzill Basics Paper; *Patterned papers:* Chatterbox, Narratives, Creative Imaginations; *Chipboard letters:* Heidi Swapp for Advantus; *Chipboard words and tabs:* Narratives, Creative Imaginations; *Rub-ons:* Art Warehouse, Creative Imaginations; *Pen:* American Crafts; *Stamp:* Paper Inspirations; *Stamping ink:* Stampin' Up!.

p. 148

THE PRETTY SISTER *by Becky Higgins* SUPPLIES *Album, metal-rimmed tag, metal frame on cover and brads:* Making Memories; *Patterned paper:* Chatterbox; *Circle punch:* EK Success; *Vellum:* Paper Adventures; *Word piece:* Li'l Davis Designs; *Ribbon:* me & my BIG ideas; *Other:* Thread.

p. 151

THE STORY OF THE SWEATER *by Lisa Russo* SUPPLIES *Patterned papers:* BasicGrey, Autumn Leaves and 7gypsies; *Brads:* American Crafts; *Rub-ons:* 7gypsies; *Metal heart:* All My Memories; *Computer fonts:* Sefia and VistaSansAlt, downloaded from the Internet.

HANDIWORK *by Becky Higgins, Photos by Vicki Allgaier* SUPPLIES *Cardstock:* Bazzill Basics Paper; *Patterned paper:* K&Company; *Paper flowers:* Prima; *Brads:* American Crafts; *Photo corners:* Heidi Swapp for Advantus; *Computer fonts:* Omatic (title), downloaded from the Internet; CK Regal, "Creative Clips & Fonts for Special Occasions" CD, *Creating Keepsakes; Chalk:* Craf-T Products.

p. 154

JOHNSON FAMILY *by Carey Johnson* SUPPLIES *Patterned paper:* My Mind's Eye; *Letter sticker:* Making Memories; *Die cuts:* Mara-Mi; *Computer fonts:* Century Gothic, Microsoft Word; Fairytale, downloaded from the Internet.

p. 156

VICTORIA'S AUTOBIOGRAPHY *by Becky Higgins* SUPPLIES *Album:* Heidi Swapp for Advantus; *Textured cardstock:* Bazzill Basics Paper; *Patterned paper:* Chatterbox; *Circle and corner-rounder punches:* EK Success; *Paper flower:* Prima; *Photo corners:* 3L; *Computer font:* Garamond, downloaded from the Internet.